HOW TO RIDE TO SMALL BUSINESS SUCCESS ON A LOW BUDGET

SALES
BEFORE
MARKETING

A straightforward 10-point process to help your business stand out and succeed!

EMMA MEHEUX

Disclaimer

Whilst this book is intended to be a source of valuable information, it is not meant to take the place of specialist advice, and readers must note that the book does not cover any legalities related to the subject matter.

The publisher, editor and author take no responsibility for any omissions or inaccuracies within the book, and hereby disclaim any liability to any party for any loss, damage or disruption that is deemed to have been caused as a consequence of reading the book.

Cover design & Illustrations by: Angela Basker Designs
Photo by: Michelle Richards Photography
Book design by: SWATT Books Ltd
Editing and proofreading by: Craig Smith (CRS Editorial)

Printed in the United Kingdom
First Printing, 2025

ISBN: 978-1-0682317-0-4 (Paperback)
ISBN: 978-1-0682317-2-8 (Hardback)
ISBN: 978-1-0682317-1-1 (eBook)

Brand Planning Books
London

www.salesbeforemarketing.com

Contents

INTRODUCTION:

CHAPTER 1:

A Cyclical Sales Approach

The Importance of Sales

Sales is one of the most important components of running a successful business. To achieve success, small business owners need to understand and embrace sales.

I don't think the sales process has changed substantially over the past few decades. I think it has simply evolved. The emergence and growth of digital has just changed the way in which sales activity needs to be done – but the underlying sales process is still very much the same as it has always been.

As far as I see it, most of the elements of the traditional sales process still exist. You just need to know how to apply these to the digital side of things, and how to take a hybrid approach of offline and online sales activity. This requires good sales planning.

To develop and promote your business effectively from a sales perspective, I believe you need to have strong sales foundations, a good sales strategy, and an understanding of the traditional sales process. You also require some knowledge of how the sales and digital marketing jigsaw fits together.

Many small businesses fail within the first few years, and often this is because of lack of income (due to a lack of sales). Sales are so important as it is the main way to drive revenue. If you really want your business to succeed, then you will have a much better chance if you give the word 'sales' the respect it deserves and incorporate sales planning into your strategic planning as soon as you can.

The Social Media Trap

I think part of the reason that small business owners often don't put enough emphasis on sales is because there is a lot of confusion between sales and marketing, and they spend too much time doing marketing activity.

Social media is a big culprit behind the reasons for this, because it's seen as a free way to market a business and make sales by many small business owners.

There are several major social media channels to choose from, where you can market your business for absolutely nothing. On these platforms you'll find a mass of marketing specialists offering free sessions to help you master social media and other forms of marketing. There is also a wealth of free information on well-known websites showing you how to market your business for free.

It sounds great in theory - as there is a sea of free knowledge and opportunities for the taking. The problem is that social media is a confusing, cluttered and competitive space and a lot of the specialists you find there are self-proclaimed specialists, with just a short course and limited experience behind them.

Sadly, many business owners get caught up for too long in the noise of social media and the free information and many 'special offers' that are of little value to them. Frequently, this results in them wasting copious amounts of time and / or money and not getting very far, results wise.

Many business owners often totally overlook the importance of sales planning and do not incorporate building strong sales foundations, or a sales strategy, into their activity.

As a result, they get caught in the 'marketing mangle' time and again. By this, I mean they go round and round in circles using free or low-cost forms of marketing (predominantly social media) until eventually they feel flat and drained from having their time, energy and budget wrung out with little return.

Once a business owner feels too drained, it can be hard for them to recover and regain the spirit required to achieve sales success.

Working Out the Costs of Social Media

A lot of small and medium-sized enterprises (SMEs) use social media as their primary marketing channel and, in my experience, many do this badly for various reasons. Also, many SMEs fail to realise the point I make about social media taking a lot of time, which has an associated cost. This point should not be overlooked as it is very important.

If you calculate the time spent planning and creating content and posting on social media and assign an hourly cost to this, you will soon see how expensive it can be. If this social media activity is not delivering enough connections or enquiries, then it's worth noting that this time may well be better spent elsewhere (such as business networking or social selling).

Let's just do a quick calculation as an example.

If you were to charge a relatively low hourly rate for a small business owner of £35 per hour and spent just 3 hours per week on social media (including content creating) that equates to £105 per week or £420 per month – or just over £5000 per year.

If your rates or the time spent are multiplied by 3 (which is highly possible) – then that's over £15,000 per year of your time.

So, you really need to ask yourself – in terms of ROI (return on investment) – is your time best spent doing social media activity, or might it be better spent doing some of the following things?

- Learning how to sell
- Planning
- Writing blogs and other, good, evergreen content
- Networking
- Social selling – using social media platforms (particularly LinkedIn) to build business relationships, and undertake other elements of sales, such as identifying prospects and developing leads
- Other sales activity.

Redressing the Balance Between Sales and Marketing

This book aims to redress the balance between sales and marketing and show how important it is that sales and marketing work in conjunction with one another. Taking things one step further, it will explain the many reasons why I believe putting sales before marketing is one of the essential keys to success for many small businesses – particularly SMEs focused on the B2B sector, providing services or high-value products.

The book will show you the importance of getting sales fundamentals right, and how combining these with good digital development / digital marketing is one of the best ways for SMEs to achieve ongoing sales success.

Essentially, *Sales Before Marketing* outlines how to secure new business by combining traditional sales processes and methods with online sales and marketing activity, particularly inbound marketing and social media marketing.

In the book I will introduce you to an easy-to-follow, unique (UniC) 10-step sales planning process that you should be able to implement cost-effectively. The book also helps demystify the complex digital landscape, and shines light on some of the low-cost marketing opportunities available that can help assist the sales process.

Strong Sales Foundations

The term 'sales foundations' is something I reference a lot in this book and in Chapter 13 I will explain what this means in detail.

However, it is important that I provide you with a brief explanation here so that you understand exactly what I am referring to when I talk about building strong sales foundations and the importance of these.

Sales foundations are all the key things that I think you need to plan and develop as soon as you possibly can if you want the best chance of being able to make sales on an ongoing basis for your business.

Building strong sales foundations is one of the 10 key elements of the UniC sales planning process and it breaks down into 8 subsidiary elements that come under the sales foundations umbrella.

These 8 points (below) are what I consider to be the 8 key things you will need to do to create strong sales foundations for your business.

I believe the stronger these foundations are, the easier it is to make sales, so these sales foundations are something that you should be continually developing and improving as your business progresses.

- Research and analysis (marketplace, competitor, SWOT analysis)
- Target audience – decision-makers, sectors and segmentation
- Brand – story, identity, values, tone of voice, and messaging
- Unique selling points (USPs)
- Product / service offering and packages
- Elevator pitches – coffee table, 60-second pitch, 3-minute pitch, 10-minute pitch
- Basic keyword and hashtag planning
- Sales literature and visuals (graphics and images).

So, Who Am I?

I'm Emma, the author, and I'm a sales, marketing, website planning, inbound marketing (e.g. SEO, PPC and content planning) specialist with an impressive 30-year career in sales and marketing. I've worked in the digital sector for approximately 25 years, pretty much since it first emerged in this country. I also have in-depth knowledge of social selling (on LinkedIn) and content writing.

I've worked for big brands and agencies, and I've sold to big brands and agencies, alongside working within and selling to the small business sector for many years.

I have a real understanding of the sales challenges small businesses face, and the difficulties they experience with both sales and digital activity. I also know how SMEs often approach sales, marketing and digital activity and how they could improve the ways they do this.

I believe that many small businesses who have low (or non-existent) marketing budgets must prioritise sales over marketing in the early years. I also think they should take a hybrid approach (online and offline) to achieve short-term sales success.

My view is that having strong sales foundations and a good sales strategy are key to long-term business success. This is because it's sales activity that can produce sufficient marketing budget to enable SMEs to undertake all sorts of marketing activities. In turn, this can help make the sales process easier, and help increase sales revenue and enable you to grow your business.

Sales planning is the main subject of this book – i.e. how to create strong sales foundations and a good sales strategy for progression so that all the sales activity, social media marketing, networking and promotional activity you do provides the best possible return on investment. After all, gaining a good ROI is generally one of the primary goals of sales and marketing.

My sales, digital marketing, SEO (search engine optimisation), website development and social selling expertise is a highly unusual and powerful combination. It's the combined experience I have in these areas that has enabled me to devise the 10-point UniC sales planning process that I introduce in this book. This process provides a structure for you to follow to gain new clients cost-effectively, and it should help you to maximise returns from your sales and marketing activities.

Why This Book Will Help You

Whatever stage you are at in your small business journey, if you are interested in attracting more clients and making more sales, then this book is for you!

If you're a budding entrepreneur or new start-up that's great, as there is no better way to create strong sales foundations than by starting with a blank canvas.

Well-established businesses who want to make more sales will also benefit from improving sales foundations and following the 10-point UniC sales planning process. So, if your organisation (or the one you work for) has been running for some time, but you're struggling to find clients and / or make sales, then this book will be extremely useful.

Sales Before Marketing will help you maximise the effectiveness of your business by covering the following important areas:

- Building strong sales foundations
- Devising a great strategy for sales growth
- Taking a hybrid approach – online and offline sales, and marketing
- Aligning your marketing / promotional strategy with your sales planning.

I believe all start-ups and SMEs should be able to do the above things in a cost-effective way. This book outlines how to do each of these things efficiently and for a low cost, with a view to helping you make more sales.

Overview of the 10-point UniC Sales Planning Process

I have devised this 10-point UniC sales planning process to help small business owners create strong sales foundations and do sales planning effectively. Each of the 10 points will be explained in detail in later chapters. I will also explain why it is called the UniC sales planning process in Chapter 9.

A quick overview of the 10 points is given below. Individually, there is nothing unusual here, but it is following the process that makes it unique.

- What's your purpose and what are your key objectives?
- Branding – naming and early branding elements (e.g. logo, design, tagline)

- Building strong sales foundations – which breaks down into 8 areas:
  - Research and analysis
  - Target audience
  - Brand identity and messaging
  - Unique selling points (USPs)
  - Product / service offering and packages
  - Elevator pitches – coffee table, 60-second pitch, 3-minute pitch, 10-minute pitch
  - Basic keyword and hashtag planning
  - Sales literature and visuals (graphics and images)

- Sales toolkit
- Networking insight and tips
- Understanding the sales process
- Overarching sales strategy / a hybrid approach
- Social media / social selling
- SEO planning
- Website planning and content.

My 10-point UniC sales planning process focuses on the importance of strong sales foundations and sales planning. By following this process from the outset, it should make sales activity and offline promotional activity easier and more effective. It should also make marketing (social media included) far less time-consuming, far more targeted, and much more likely to deliver a good return on investment.

Leaky Bucket Syndrome

As previously mentioned, I think too many small businesses spend way too much time and energy on social media and other low-cost marketing methods without achieving the returns they hope for.

This is because if you don't have strong sales foundations or a good strategic approach to sales (i.e. sales planning), social media and marketing activity can be compared to pouring liquid into a bucket with holes in. Much of the time and effort you invest (which equates to money) leaks out of the bottom.

So, a lot of the posting you are currently doing on social media could be wasted if you do not have a strategic sales-focused approach.

One of the primary objectives of the 10-point UniC sales planning process is to help business owners glue up the holes in their buckets (or ideally, start out with a bucket without holes). In other words, create strong sales foundations and a strategy to nurture and grow sales by ensuring your marketing bucket retains enough liquid to water important sales seeds, instead of leaking out over all the weeds.

By watering weeds, you're not only wasting your marketing efforts but you're also encouraging them to grow, making it harder for you to see through them and get to the sales seeds (i.e. great prospects).

If you can create a bucket with as few holes as possible, then any marketing / social media, sales or promotional activity you do is likely to be far more effective and produce a much better ROI (return on investment). This is because it will retain more liquid which will enable you to keep watering and nurturing sales seeds.

Once regular sales are coming in, you should be in a much better position to dedicate a sufficient monthly budget to the ongoing digital development and marketing that's required to generate consistent inbound enquiries.

So, if you do your early sales planning right, it should put you on the road to future success with your venture.

The Importance of Inbound Marketing in Relation to Sales

Inbound marketing refers to marketing methods used to help you generate incoming visitors and sales enquiries to your business, and often to your website.

Aside from social media, there are all sorts of great opportunities on the digital marketing side, but these often take a reasonable level of financial investment / budget (e.g. SEO – which will probably be a monthly fee of £500 or more when using good specialists) – and are likely to have associated costs (e.g. web development). This type of price point can be too prohibitive for many small business owners to invest in early on.

So, if your marketing budget is low at the outset, getting sales flowing as quickly as possible, cheaply, will unlock the door to you being able to start inbound marketing. This is because you will be able to create a marketing budget from revenue gained from early sales and allocate this to various forms of marketing.

Doing inbound marketing should be beneficial as things such as SEO and PPC (pay per click) are particularly good ways to generate quality sales leads. This is because they are highly targeted forms of marketing that attract visitors when they are searching – i.e. when they are looking for keywords relevant to your business and its products or services.

Generating inbound enquiries on an ongoing basis is a fantastic position to be in because these types of enquirers have come from search, or from seeing content you have distributed, and are often in 'buying mode'. This means they're likely to be responsive to sales discussions, which in turn makes sales easier to close.

Another thing to note in relation to this is that all forms of inbound marketing activity (SEO, PPC, content marketing etc.) produce far better results if strong sales foundations are in place and the inbound marketing has been planned strategically to work in line with the sales foundations and sales planning.

This is another reason why following the 10-point UniC sales planning process is so beneficial, as laying strong foundations for inbound activity to be implemented (at a date when you can afford to do so) is a very good strategy for longer-term gain. For example, you need a good website and / or landing page(s) for SEO and PPC to work well. However, if planned well from the outset, you could have these elements built relatively cost-effectively early on before you have to spend on the other associated costs for SEO or PPC. It's just really thinking ahead of the game (as it were) and this can save you time and money in the long run.

It's a Cyclical-style Sales Approach

Producing sales as quickly as possible will also open the door to you being able to allocate more time to other forms of low-cost or free marketing too such as video creation, podcasts, events, presentations, eBooks and even book writing etc. You can potentially do some of these things yourself, or by hiring affordable suppliers, but these things take time.

If you are the owner of your business and the main salesperson too, then you will probably only have spare time available to focus on other things once sales are coming in and being serviced effectively. This is one good reason why following the 10-step process to help you make sales as quickly as possible is so advantageous.

Once sales start coming from early sales activity and / or inbound enquiries, it should free up your time to do all sorts of other forms of low-cost marketing and promotion that are freely available options but time-consuming to do.

In turn, this should lead to more sales. Essentially, it's a cyclical-style sales and marketing approach:

Initial sales (from offline and online sales activity)
↳ marketing budget
↳ digital marketing activity (e.g. SEO / PPC)
↳ incoming sales enquiries
↳ sales from incoming marketing AND continual sales work
↳ more time availability AND more sales
↳ time for free / more cost-effective forms of marketing (e.g. content creation, podcast appearances)
↳ more sales
↳ more marketing budget

...and so it continues.

Who This Book is Aimed At

The terms 'small business' and 'SMEs' apply to all manner of companies. Some can be quite sizeable in terms of turnover and number of employees, but this book focuses on a specific subset – businesses that tend to be on the smaller side and that operate locally, or within a specific geographic area – e.g. London. So, when I use the terms 'SME' and 'small business', this is the type of business I am referring to.

Whilst the content of *Sales Before Marketing* will be useful for many businesses, the SMEs I have in mind when writing are the type of privately owned businesses found in local areas. These can range from sole traders, solopreneurs and microbusinesses (with only a few employees) to businesses with more staff – but generally, the typical types of companies you are likely to meet at local business / networking events.

Some of the common traits of such businesses are:

- They are likely to be based and operating within a local area or a specific section of the country – sometimes they will provide a nationwide service, but more often than not they will be geographically focused (due to costs of service provision, delivery etc.)
- Their annual turnover is estimated at being typically between £10,000 and £2 million (although this could be a lot higher)
- They are service-based businesses or those selling high-value products (e.g. garden rooms or furniture)
- They have limited budget for marketing / promotional activity – usually less than £5000 per month, often less than £500 per month, and frequently under £200 per month
- They have a very small sales team – often only an owner / manager sales team, or a team of just one or two people.

The ideal type of small business I have in mind is one looking to generate service leads or high-value product leads – e.g. garden rooms, furniture, or hot tubs. This can be for 'business to business' (B2B) or 'business to consumer' (B2C) markets, but it is more often going to apply to B2B.

The annual value of the lead is likely to be £1000 plus, with potential for much higher lifetime client value.

It's important to note that for businesses that require high-volume sales of low-cost products / services – e.g. books, courses, tickets and / or mainly provide online services – that different sales and marketing techniques are likely to be required – more of a digital-first approach.

Whilst many of the points covered in this book will be useful for these types of businesses too, they are not the businesses this book is aimed at. High-volume sales of low-cost items do tend to require more marketing, and social media activity is likely to deliver better results for the sale of low-cost items.

The Main Points This Book Covers

- Why a strong brand is so important for businesses, and what is involved in sales-focused branding
- What the term 'sales' means and why sales are so important
- The differences between sales and marketing
- Why sales planning is so important
- Why sales should come before marketing
- Insight into how to develop strong sales foundations
- What's likely to be involved in the sales foundation and sales planning work
- Why purpose and values are important for sales
- Why digital materials are so important when it comes to sales (i.e. domain name, website, social media pages, digital sales material)
- How to create and deliver a great elevator pitch
- An overview of the traditional sales process and the key elements of this

- How these key elements from the traditional sales process translate to digital
- Insight into business networking and the important role this plays in modern sales
- Networking etiquette and how to network effectively
- Marketing planning – why a strategic approach, which is aligned to the sales planning strategy, is so important for high-quality digital sales enquiries to be produced
- An overview of the main types of local marketing that SMEs could do to enhance sales results
- Insight into SEO, a highly targeted form of marketing that can be very beneficial for sales
- How to align the different forms of inbound marketing and local marketing to your sales planning
- An outline of the sales, marketing and digital mix (i.e. how sales, marketing and digital need to function together and how they can complement each other for best sales results)
- How advertising fits into the mix
- An in-depth explanation of why a website is so important and how it sits centrally to most other forms of sales and marketing
- Insight into social selling and how to use this as a bridge between offline and online sales activity.

The primary focus of this book is about improving sales through sales planning, and it will highlight six key things throughout.

- Why foundational sales work and getting the basics right is so important
- Why sales should come before marketing
- What sales is and how to do it effectively and for low-cost
- Why having a process and strategy to follow is important
- Why keeping things simple works well for SMEs
- Why marketing needs to be aligned to a sales strategy for best results.

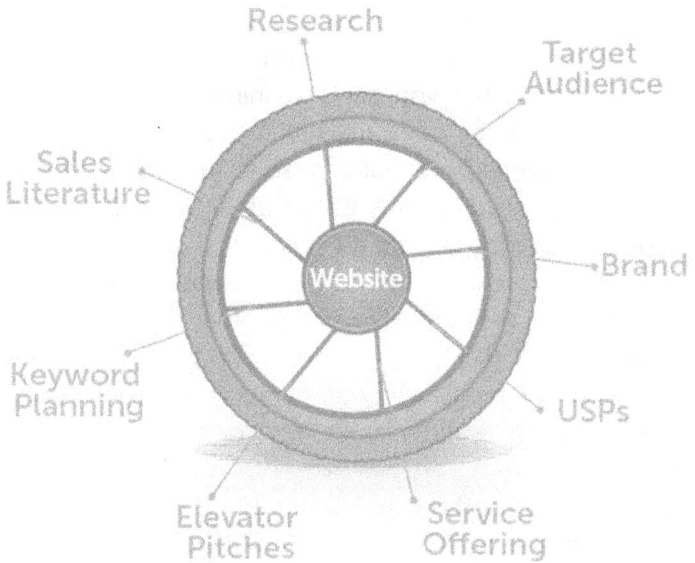

Research

Target Audience

Sales Literature

Website

Brand

Keyword Planning

USPs

Elevator Pitches

Service Offering

CHAPTER 2:

Some Sales Lessons

Now I'm going to tell you a bit about me, why I'm so well qualified to write this book and why I've written the book.

I've included this chapter for two reasons.

- To value this book, you need to believe that I truly know what I'm talking about when it comes to sales and marketing, and that I have the credentials for the book to be of value to you.

- Every business owner should have a clear idea of what drives them, what they are working towards and why they are doing it – i.e. What is their 'purpose'? Giving you some insight into what drives me, and what my purpose is, will allow you to get to know me better, and it may also help you think about and explore these things too.

I think knowing your purpose is an integral element of the sales process for small business owners. This is because if you know what you want to achieve, it makes planning how to achieve it that much easier.

Starting Out in Sales

I cut my teeth in sales in Saturday jobs, and by the time I was 17 years old, I had already recognised I was naturally rather good at it. I think this became very clear to me the day that I managed to sell a man with one leg an expensive wooden shoe tree for the shoe he was never going to use!

He was so impressed with my sales ability, he not only bought the shoe tree, but also an additional pair of shoes, and all the shoe polish and shoe care accessories I could sell him. As he left the shop, he turned around and smiled, and told me that I could go a long way in a media sales career.

I'll always remember that day, as his words about the glitzy world of media stayed firmly in my mind for months and were the catalyst for my long-standing sales career.

By 18, I had done it. I had landed myself a media sales job for a big newspaper group. It was a graduate role, but I wasn't a graduate, and I was elated.

I succeeded because I had copious amounts of drive and tenacity at that age, and I was so determined to get a graduate role and get into media without going to university, that I just went for it. However, in hindsight, it's easy to see I had five major things going for me when I was looking to secure my first sales role.

- **Self-belief** – I firmly believed I could do it.
- **Product knowledge** – I was the product (in this instance), and I was prepared to sell my strengths and their benefits because I firmly believed in what I was selling.
- **Communication skills** – I was good at talking, asking questions, listening to answers and adapting my response accordingly.

- **Tenacity** – I was prepared to push boundaries until I succeeded.
- **Resilience** – I was not going to give up, no matter how hard things got.

I now realise that these attributes show that I had a natural aptitude for sales. This is because these are five integral things that all salespeople require if they are going to sell successfully.

When I was 18, the first of these attributes that I used to my advantage to secure my first role was tenacity. For 2 days I knocked on door after door of every media sales recruitment agency I could find in London. Eventually, after numerous receptionists had refused me entry, one door opened!

The media sales roles these recruitment agencies had on their books were ALL graduate only. This is why it was so very hard to get my foot in the door.

Thinking back, I now realise it was that early door-knocking experience that is probably one of the first impactful lessons I learnt when it comes to sales. I recognised very early on that to be good in sales, you must be prepared to put yourself in front of a lot of people and get lots of rejections before you get a 'Yes'.

I also recognised that making sales takes time, and I quickly realised that you need a very thick skin to do well!

Sales is a Numbers Game

I was subsequently taught by professional sales trainers that sales is a numbers game. The more doors you knock on, the more chance you have of someone saying 'Yes' and making the sale. I kept on knocking when many others would have given up and that's why, when one door finally opened, I was given a chance.

All those doors slamming in my face did not phase me. For your business to succeed at sales, you and / or your team will need to find that tenacity and resilience too, as I firmly believe the early sales training I received was right, and that sales is a numbers game.

It may not involve knocking on physical doors these days, but you still need to somehow deliver a good sales message to enough of the right type of people – whether that's through online or offline means. Ideally, it should be a combination of both.

The more quality prospects you deliver the message to, the closer you'll be moving towards getting a 'Yes', but you'll also receive a lot of rejections along the way. Ever since my early door-knocking days, I look at this process with a positive slant – i.e. the more rejections you get, the better, as eventually you'll reach enough rejections for there to be a tipping point where the seesaw lands in the sales gold sandpit. No-one can say how many rejections this will take as it depends on so many things.

A Sales Mindset

One thing that is very important if you want to be successful at sales is having the right mindset. There are all sorts of things you can employ here, but one thing I think it's very worthwhile remembering is that you will get rejections time and again. So don't look at sales that don't happen in a negative light – instead, look at it as I do, like you're on a long walk in icy conditions and each 'No' you get is just leading you that bit closer to a log cabin full of warmth.

Over the years, my prospects and clients have included some of the most well-known brands you can think of. I've sold digital services and non-digital services, and I've also managed various teams of salespeople very successfully.

Whatever I have sold, and whoever I have been selling for (or to), I know that many of the fundamental and foundational elements of the sales process have not changed in the 30 plus years I've been in sales.

One of the most important lessons that I learnt as part of this process is that every 'No' leads you closer to a 'Yes'. To be good at sales I believe you need to truly get on board with this way of thinking.

You need to equip yourself with a mindset full of positivity, determination and resilience, as otherwise rejections could prove to be too difficult to handle.

My First Elevator Pitch

Back in the late eighties, after 2 days of persevering, when I was finally given a chance to speak with a recruitment consultant, he quickly set me a rather unusual task.

He asked me to sell him a piece of dry bread and gave me just 2 minutes to do this!

It was a hot summer's day, in a small top floor office, above the busy sounds of Regent Street, where I delivered my first-ever elevator pitch with absolute perfection!

This was another pivotal and memorable moment in my sales journey, and I felt like a footballer scoring from midfield. I'd started out with a very low chance of success, but I was focused on the goal and kicked the ball so hard with absolute precision. I also put such a good spin on it that it landed neatly in the top corner of the net.

My elevator pitch had done it! I wanted to stand up and run around the swivel chair that I was sat on waving my hands in the air shouting – GOAL!! But I didn't – I just smiled the smile that was set to take me a long way in sales and took hold of the job specs being handed to me.

What I had achieved with my inaugural elevator pitch was make an imaginary piece of dry bread sound so enticing that by the time the 2 minutes were up, both the consultant and I were almost drooling.

I wanted to take a big bite of the imaginary toast I'd conjured up and so did he. I had quite literally turned a dry piece of bread into a golden, sumptuous snack, dripping in warm butter and honey, fresh from the oven, with a wholesome, homely aroma wafting from it. You could see the toast, smell it, and taste it, and it wasn't even there. More than that, you wanted it, because the description of it was so good it made you realise you had a hungry hole to fill that you didn't previously know existed.

That's what I believe good sales ability is ultimately about – drawing a picture in someone's mind that makes them realise they have a need they may not even know about. Then showing them how your product / service will solve that need AND benefit them greatly. These days it can be done by offline or online means – ideally both.

Key Points for Good Elevator Pitch Delivery

Elevator pitches are a very important tool in sales, and I explain a lot more about these later in the book, but I want to start by explaining a few points now that relate to that first-ever elevator pitch I did.

My experience over the years has shown me that to succeed at elevator pitch delivery, you need to act like a footballer (just like I did all those years ago) and deliver when on the pitch, by systematically doing the following:

- Know your target.
- Focus on the target and how you are going to score.
- Aim for a great delivery.
- Put your weight behind it.
- Kick it right across the field (or audience).
- Put great spin on it.
- And score with a goal they won't forget – i.e. make it memorable.

I've gone on to do exceptionally well in several types of sales roles throughout my career and in one way or another, elevator pitches have always been a prerequisite to getting in the door to do a longer pitch.

In fact, elevator pitches have always been an integral part of the traditional sales process, but I think this is one element of sales that has become more important over time.

This is primarily because networking (online and offline) has become more widely used as a way of finding prospects and building and nurturing business relationships, and ultimately making sales. In essence, networking has become one widely accepted way of old style 'cold-calling' because it's where you can pitch directly to new people (potential prospects). A good elevator pitch can have an incredibly positive impact on networking success and that's one key reason why a good elevator pitch is so important these days. I will explain more about elevator pitches in Chapters 13 and 15.

The Importance of Effective Targeting

Whilst I do believe there is a lot of truth in the saying that sales is a numbers game, another one of my very early lessons was learning that getting in front of the right type of people is key – i.e. targeting effectively is of paramount importance.

> There's no doubt in my mind that the better you target your audience, the more successful you're likely to be, and good targeting undoubtedly comes down to good sales planning. I think this point is more important now than it has ever been. This is because the small business market is far more competitive than ever.

I'd much rather deliver a sales message to 100 people that are the right type of prospects than 1000 people that are totally random. So, knocking on the right doors is incredibly important, or alternatively getting the right people to knock on your door (via SEO, PPC and well-planned social media activity). This is the quality over quantity approach and something I think is vital for small business success.

> The 10-point UniC sales planning process I have created is heavily focused on effective sales targeting, and the strategic approach I suggest for early marketing activity for SMEs is always a highly targeted approach.

Regardless of what you are selling, or who to, I believe the better your sales planning, targeting, sales messaging and sales pitch delivery, the better conversion rate you'll have. This has always been the case – things here have not changed.

What has changed over the years is the sales distribution channels and the methods in which sales messages are delivered. Cold-calling by phone is not widely used in B2B sales within the small business market anymore. Instead, this has been replaced by things like networking and social selling which are essentially different ways of cold-calling – because you can still speak to potential prospects that you have never met before by using these methods.

Get the Sales Prospects Coming to You

Getting people knocking on your door via inbound marketing techniques – i.e. SEO, PPC, and content marketing etc. is also a great way to find new clients. These techniques only work well if there are good sales foundations in place in the first instance though, and of course a door!

I think that sales strategy should be closely intertwined with your inbound marketing strategy. In fact, I don't believe you can do inbound marketing very effectively unless it is done in conjunction with sales strategy and sales planning.

Whilst you'll still have to knock on a lot of doors or get people knocking on your door (as it were), the more of these doors that open and allow you to interact with the prospect the other side, the more chance you'll have of sales success. This, however, is only true if your sales foundations and messaging are strong. I also believe the best form of interaction once the door is open is face-to-face – ideally in-person – but if this is not possible then by phone or video call.

Your website and / or well-written landing pages or social media pages will be what act as entry points (doors) to visitors. The better and more professional your website and other key landing pages are, the easier it will be for quality prospects to find the doorbell (as it were) so they can ring it (i.e. submit warm enquiries) and let you know they are there waiting to be seen.

Once you answer the door by responding to an enquiry, this is the point at which the call can be taken back offline or to a video meeting, whereby the traditional sales process can be followed.

Find the Right Balance

The foundational elements of the traditional sales process have not changed much but digital has mixed things up an awful lot. How you maximise sales returns using a combination of old school sales tactics and digital prowess is something that I will endeavour to cover in this book. It's not the easiest subject to explain as some of the digital side is full of complexity, but it's not rocket science either. I hope that I explain it in an easy-to-understand manner.

Whilst the old school sales lessons I learnt so well remain firmly in place, how sales are made continues to evolve and digital has impacted (and continues to impact) sales in a big way. What has certainly changed is how sales are made and what sales tools and channels are available to SMEs to help make sales.

Finding the right balance between sales and marketing is hard. As a lot depends on budget and resources, it will differ immensely for different companies. For example, the more budget there is, the easier it is to use different forms of inbound marketing and other digital marketing to drive quality enquiries / sales.

However, in my view, building strong sales foundations and devising a good sales-focused strategy should always come first and foremost. This applies to businesses of all sizes, as all businesses need these things for best results. Bigger companies just have the advantage of being able to invest far more heavily in different forms of digital marketing earlier on.

For small B2B businesses with low marketing budgets (under 1k per month), the 10-point UniC sales planning process should be very helpful in providing an idea of how to do low-cost sales planning and obtain a good balance of sales and marketing both short-term and longer-term.

By following the 10-point UniC sales planning process you should also be able to generate sales revenue relatively quickly, some of which can be put aside for marketing – this is what triggers the cyclical element of the cyclical-style approach that this planning process is based on.

What is My Purpose?

My purpose is very much based around having a good work / life balance and avoiding too much stress.

I want a business that meets the above criteria whilst allowing me to achieve some of the things I want to achieve.

I also want to develop my business into one that allows me to use my expertise and past experiences to help raise awareness of mental health issues – and this is partly due to experiences I've had during my own business journey.

I know small business owners and senior level executives can end up experiencing mental health crises because of a multitude of reasons. The reasons can often be associated with 'sales' in one way or another – lack of sales / lack of cash flow and scaling up being major areas of stress for many business owners.

Making sales isn't easy, scaling businesses certainly isn't easy, and running a small business can be exceptionally hard at times for a lot of people, as can running sales and marketing teams when in senior level roles.

Why Knowing Your Purpose is So Important in Relation to Sales

One of the first things I explain to clients is that as small business owners we all need to have a 'purpose'. Why are we doing what we are doing? What do we want to achieve from it? – i.e. what does success look like to us?

Once we know this, we can work out both our personal and business objectives. This is important to work out as it is not very easy to start sales planning or set sales objectives or KPIs (key performance indicators) until we know these two things.

Some Snippets of My Story

For much of my working life, I was referred to as a workaholic by those that knew me well – which is not really a good thing. But I continually worked extremely hard because I wanted to succeed.

For decades, achieving success financially was my number one goal, but no matter how hard I worked I didn't manage to achieve this objective. Not through lack of sales I hasten to add – but various hurdles that got in my way. In fact, you could say that being too good at sales was in some ways problematic for me as growing a business and scaling it into a much bigger business led to a multitude of difficulties, in all sorts of ways.

By 2015 I'd failed hard in business. I'd also held some very pressurised senior level sales / marketing roles for well-known brands, and I'd experienced unexpected and unwanted job losses along the way.

The Treadmill

For over 25 years, I'd kept on pushing myself forward, and I had been under continual work-related pressures. However, no matter how hard I worked, I seemed to be trapped on some sort of imaginary treadmill.

I kept running as fast as I could but not really getting anywhere and I just seemed to get thrown off time and time again – yet each time, I just got straight back up, jumped on the treadmill again and ran even faster.

That was up until 2015, when a spate of very difficult events, both work wise and personally, coupled with the pressure of never slowing down, finally mounted up into a meltdown of my mental health.

I hit a tall, hard, solid, wall incredibly hard – something that's commonly known as burnout, or a breakdown. Couple this with some pre-existing neurodiverse challenges that got harder to manage having hit the wall, and I became exceptionally poorly for quite some time.

Panic attacks, depression, a severe anxiety disorder and other neurodiverse traits made life virtually impossible to manage and completely unbearable. Anxiety issues that I had managed to control for years suddenly became very much out of control as everything rose to the surface at once. I cannot explain how incredibly frightening and difficult this period of my life was, but that story is for another book another time.

What I will say, is that it was almost impossible for me to function, and I don't know to this day how I got through it. I can't even write too much about it, as it's almost a decade on and the memories are still too triggering, traumatic and painful. I just know I was very lucky to have some people around me that really cared, and a fantastic counsellor. I was also lucky to be someone that had always persevered and always had a lot of resilience, and somehow, I managed to drag myself over the wall.

As I slowly started to get better, I knew I had to reassess the way I worked. Mental health issues also meant analysing what I really wanted to achieve in life. Once I knew this, I had to decide how I was going to get there. It was about having a purpose - knowing what I wanted to do and why

It required a real shift in mindset in terms of what I wanted to achieve, and what the most important things to me were. It also meant coming out of my comfort zone and learning to work in a very different style to the manner I had been used to.

In 2016, I left the treadmill behind for good and I took time to reflect. If I hadn't done so, my story could be a very much darker and different story as I think my treadmill could have quite literally hurled me into oblivion. If I'm honest, for a short amount of time, I felt like it already had!

Changing Route

So, I totally changed course back in the spring of 2016. I chose to stop working in central London in senior level full-time roles, and I started working part-time locally for a small agency. This allowed me to take time to look after myself and my wellbeing and continue to go to weekly counselling sessions, which I did for 18 months.

Having made the transformation, I soon realised I was 10 times happier than I had been previously, and I have never regretted choosing lifestyle and values over the race for money and success!

The irony is that I never wanted material goods in the first place. It was freedom to make choices, the ambition to achieve the key things I wanted, the time to do more of the things that made me happy, and the desire to do something that would positively impact others that had pushed me on for all those years.

By changing direction, I instantly got provided with something I had not previously had, and that was time!

For once, I had time to take a proper step back and just think. After some serious soul searching, I realised I just had to be clever and find a different way to achieve the same things I'd always been striving for.

So, from 2016 onwards, I built myself up mentally and emotionally and I built my knowledge and connections up too. I even built my personal and social life up – and eventually went on to start running my own very small local business at the beginning of 2020 – Brand Planning – brandplanning.co.uk

The change in 2016 also gave me time to do one thing I had always wanted to do – write! – and since then writing and learning about publishing books has been a big focus for me.

EMMA MEHEUX | www.salesbeforemarketing.com

I still work very hard, and I still have goals work wise, but now I do things in my time without the high-level of stress that I previously had.

I also found that I thoroughly enjoy working with (and alongside) small business owners locally, and community is one of the values I now class very highly on my values list.

Setting Realistic Expectations

I don't want to grow my small business into a bigger business with lots of employees as I've been there, done that, and I know what trials, tribulations and trauma that can bring.

I also know that due to the fragility of my mental health I must look after that first and foremost, and for me, that means avoiding high levels of stress.

I'm happy to keep my business as a tiny business and focus on my other values and hobbies too, which include creativity (particularly writing).

Learning from the challenges I've faced in the past, and using my story and experiences to help others, is a key thing that now propels me forward.

What Does Success Mean to You?

One thing I've realised over recent years, is that running a business means very different things for different people and you will need to decide what it means to you.

For me it's about a few things – communication, community, charity, creativity, flexibility and freedom. Financially it's just about generating a reasonable income for myself. So, my business is very much a lifestyle business. I know that, and I'm happy with that, and my sales strategy works in accordance with it.

If my creative side leads to future financial gain to allow me more freedom, more choice and more ability to do the things I want then great – but if not, that's fine too. At least I can enjoy the journey and remain true to my values.

For you – your business can be whatever you want it to be, but first and foremost you need to know your 'purpose' and form your business planning and sales planning around the objectives that are associated with this.

> Defining your personal, financial, business and sales objectives should be some of the first things you do as part of the sales planning process. This is because you need to clearly define your goals to plan how you will achieve them!

You can't sell effectively if you don't have sales targets. But you can't set achievable targets if you don't know what you need to achieve sales-wise or how you plan to achieve it. To do this, you need a clear idea of your purpose and key objectives.

Knowing your purpose and objectives can be a fluid thing too – these can change over time, but having a clear idea of what they are for the next 2 years is a great place to start.

Looking After Your Wellbeing

Hopefully, if you work out your purpose and follow a well-thought-out sales planning strategy that is aligned to your objectives and budget, you should make a great success of your business.

But there is no doubt that it is not always easy, and most business owners will experience difficulties at different times in their business journey – some more difficult than others.

Wanting to build and grow a business and striving for success is admirable, but it's hard work, and as far as I'm concerned nothing is more important than your health and wellbeing. So, I try and encourage all business owners to take good care of their health (particularly mental health) and their wellbeing too.

I think it's important to take time out daily to focus on your wellbeing. I also think regular holidays (breaks) are vital to help you recharge mentally, physically and emotionally.

No matter how busy you are, you should be able to find some time each day to focus on you, and even if you're struggling to make the business work there should still be time in a day to look after your wellbeing.

Walking is something that works for me. I love walking and soaking up the beauty of the nature around me. I think this is immensely valuable for mental and physical health.

Different things work for different people though, so you could prefer the gym or running or swimming, or something creative like art or writing. The point I'm making is that I think it's very important to make time in your day for something like this. If you don't, and you just focus on business / work (like I made the mistake of doing for years), this approach could have health ramifications like it did for me!

Also, there should be no reason why you can't take a proper break at some point in the year. You don't have to go away, just take a break from work for a week or more.

If the Going Gets Tough

If the going does get too tough, I also think it's well worth remembering a few of the lessons that I have learnt over time. If you are aware of these, hopefully you won't have to learn the hard way like I did!

- Mental health matters a lot!
- Failing does not make you a failure.
- If the road you're on is not rewarding, there are other routes.
- Be prepared to pivot if need be.
- Take joy from the journey.
- Getting out is not the same as giving up.

Communication and Connections

Running your own business can be very hard however small your business is – there are all sorts of challenges at different levels. Working alone can be tough too, and setting the bar too high can be problematic.

So, knowing your purpose and key objectives, and creating a strategic approach that enables you to go at the right pace for you, are things that I think all business owners should plan for.

> I also think getting out and about and communicating with other small business owners can be the lifeline that a lot of people need. Going it alone might sound like fun, but I think going it alone with others to lean on when you need to, is a whole lot better!

If you want to build a business or grow your existing business into one with quite a few employees and a high growth plan, then that's great, and it could potentially work well for you and have a very positive outcome.

However, there are pitfalls you need to be aware of, and I'd say you should have a good business plan and a well-thought-out sales and marketing strategy in place to do this effectively.

There are lots of good specialists around in local areas who charge reasonable rates, and these are some of the areas you may want to consider working with specialists on.

- Business planning
- Coaching
- Sales
- Marketing
- Logistics and operations
- Digital development
- Mentoring
- Financial planning.

If you just want to have a tiny business like me, that's fine too. But whatever size your business is, one thing is for sure, you will need to understand the sales process and find ways to sell effectively if you want to gain new clients on a regular basis.

So, working with sales and marketing specialists is one of the first things I think you should do too. Find people that you trust, with experience, and learn from them! In addition, I'd say try and be realistic with your expectations, and your limitations.

There are also several fantastic organisations that help start-up entrepreneurs and small business owners with lots of free opportunities to meet specialists, attend workshops etc. You'll find a list of some London ones on the Brand Planning website – brandplanning.co.uk/business-resources

In Summary

So now you know a bit more about my background, my credentials, my purpose and some of the things I am passionate about.

I will be so pleased if you find this book helpful, and if you can apply some of the sales and marketing tips to your business effectively, that would be fantastic.

I'll be just as pleased if this one section of the book gives you some insight into how important it is to know what you want to achieve, and to take care of yourself on your business journey.

I hope that reading *Sales Before Marketing* will give you valuable insight into the importance of sales planning and help you to grow and flourish in business.

PART 1:

SALES PLANNING

CHAPTER 3:

Why Sales Planning Matters

Some of the Sales and Marketing Problems SMEs Experience

Before I explain the main differences that I think there are between sales and marketing, I thought it would be useful to list some typical issues I see small business owners experiencing in relation to making sales (or not making sales – to be more accurate).

Do you resonate with any of these?

Why not go through this list and seriously think about how many apply to you.

- They don't think they need to sell – social media is enough
- They don't like selling
- They have never been taught how to sell
- They don't like networking

- They have no sales planning strategy
- They lack sales direction
- They are overflowing with ideas but don't know where to start, sales-wise
- They are not quite sure what they are selling
- They don't know their USPs
- They think networking doesn't work for them
- They find networking is too time-consuming
- They don't follow up with contacts after networking events
- They don't want to niche – they are convinced their audience is every other small business
- The word 'sales' does not sit well with them – it brings up bad connotations
- They lack confidence with networking and / or sales
- They don't think you need to sell these days – they believe it can all be done by marketing
- They have ideas how to improve sales, but don't know where to start
- They don't have sales packages
- They are not sure how to package their service offering
- They don't know how to price their service offering
- They have too many other things to do to allocate time to sales
- They don't have sales materials
- They don't think they need sales materials
- They don't have a sales pipeline
- They don't want to move from their comfort zone (often social media)
- They don't put any value on sales
- They think things are just difficult generally sales-wise due to economy or similar things
- They think inbound marketing (SEO, PPC etc.) is too expensive
- SEO didn't work in the past, so they think it won't work in the future

- They think SEO is too complicated or expensive to get sales from it
- They don't believe they need to spend much time or money on a website
- They don't think they need a website at all
- They haven't got a good brand or brand strategy
- They feel like they're going round in circles on social media
- They find social media is too competitive
- They think social media is becoming way too time-consuming
- They think paid social media advertising doesn't work
- They don't have any budget for paid marketing
- They suffer from imposter syndrome
- They don't like promoting themselves as part of the sales / marketing process
- Social media isn't producing good enough results
- They are downhearted and despondent
- They are totally confused by sales and marketing
- They just do what they see others do
- They don't know how to change things
- They don't think they have the budget to make improvements
- They continue doing the same things and they continue getting poor results.

The 7-point Glitch

It seems to me that the last 7 points listed above are often the position in which a lot of small business owners find themselves after 2-3 years in business. I call this dangerous time the 7-point glitch. It's dangerous because if small business owners don't find a way to turn the glitch into a hitch, then this can be the point at which things really start to go downhill.

It's the time a small business owner tends to reach when they may have tried various things to improve sales by trying to address many of the other points listed, but to no avail. I believe this is usually because they haven't put any form of strategic sales planning in place and because of the very last point – they continue doing the same things that aren't working (such as social media posts), and they continue getting poor results.

Three of the biggest problems that I continually see that lead business owners to reach this stage are:

- People don't understand how to differentiate between sales and marketing, and overlook the sales piece.
- They are really confused at how to do marketing effectively – this is partly because there is just so much choice of marketing opportunities that it is overwhelming.
- They follow the crowd and believe things they hear on social media – e.g. it's good to do things consistently. This is a great example, as 'Yes', it is good to have consistency if what you are doing consistently is constantly good – if it's not good though, you will continually be doing the wrong things, which will be having a detrimental effect on progress as opposed to a positive impact.

So, if small business owners had a better understanding of the differences between sales and marketing and the importance of the sales elements earlier on, I think it would make a very positive impact for many businesses.

For existing businesses, the good news is it's never too late to learn. Sales planning can be done at anytime, and what you have in place already can always be adapted to incorporate new sales-focused strategies.

The 10-point UniC sales planning process should help give you an in-depth overview of the sales side. In Part 2 of the book, I provide much more detailed information on how to improve the sales side of things. But in the following pages I will try and untangle sales and marketing as a whole and give some clarity on this subject.

What is Sales Planning?

The following paragraph is my summary of sales planning:

Sales planning helps to create strong sales foundations and a solid sales strategy, which, in turn, helps maximise return on investment from marketing and promotional activity. Without good sales planning, the time and / or budget spent on marketing can be wasted.

As this book progresses it will:

- explain what sales planning is
- explain why sales planning is so important
- explain how you can undertake sales planning effectively and cost-effectively
- explain what makes strong sales foundations
- explain what a sales development strategy involves
- explain the main types of marketing activity SMEs with low budgets can do to assist sales development, once strong sales foundations are in place.

Forget the Bells and Whistles

Another issue I see regularly with small businesses in relation to sales and marketing is they want to run before they can walk.

There is so much talk about AI, cutting-edge technology, the latest software packages, advanced SEO etc. and people get carried away with the idea of these things and overlook the sales basics.

I'm a firm believer that the super techy stuff should just be the bells and whistles. Think of it like a car with all the top-of-the-range latest gadgets. These are fine if you can afford them and know how to use them effectively. But if your car has no ability to move (i.e. functioning wheels), it doesn't matter how many bells and whistles you add, you still won't get very far!

If you are a small business owner wanting to make more sales, I suggest stepping away from the noise. Stop thinking you must do everything and / or know about all the latest sales and marketing trends – just focus on some of the core fundamentals first.

The fundamentals of sales have not changed for decades. We simply have different distribution channels and delivery routes than we had 20 years ago – there are lots of them and things are changing and advancing at an extremely fast rate. But you simply cannot use all these delivery routes straight away, and ensuring the wheels of the vehicle are firmly in place first is the thing that is of paramount importance.

First and foremost, a good grasp of sales and marketing fundamentals and building strong sales foundations is what gets the wheels turning most quickly for SMEs looking to gain sales traction. Add an excellent strategy and good sales activity, and this is the fuel that enables small SME vehicles to compete against the supercars!

Once racing nicely, then you can add the gadgets and gizmos that make things look good and go faster if you want. Until then, it should really be about getting on the road and into the race, and it is quite simply wheels and fuel that will allow you to do this and not all the flashy stuff.

So, whenever you think of trialling the latest hi-tech stuff, I suggest you ask yourself this question:

What would be the benefit of having the latest top-of-the-range navigation system in a vehicle, if you can't even get the wheels to go round?

The Importance of Sales Planning

Sales activity and digital development working in conjunction with one another is particularly important when it comes to generating sales and is something all small business owners should think about as soon as possible. I believe sales planning is crucial for these areas to work together effectively and deliver good results. Ideally you want to add marketing into the mix too once you have the budget to do so, and so future marketing activity should be thought about at the sales planning stage too.

Having a good sales planning strategy is becoming more and more important for SMEs in the B2B sector for many reasons:

- Social media has become incredibly busy.
- Competition is fierce across most sectors and channels — particularly social media.
- Low budgets make digital success harder.
- Sales success generally requires focus and intent.
- Understanding how the digital jigsaw fits together is important.

- Good strategic planning allows content to be repurposed more easily.
- Inbound enquiries are the best – but you absolutely need a strategy for successful inbound marketing.
- A hybrid approach – offline and online – can be great for SMEs but requires good planning to maximise sales results.

It's best to try and use specialists as early on as possible to help you with strategic planning, but there are elements you can start working on yourself too.

Some Sales Planning Points to Ponder

If you want to start doing some sales planning yourself, here are a few tips to get started.

- Strategic planning starts with analysing where you are.
- Give yourself time to think about where you want to go.
- Try and work out who your target audience is and then refine this further.
- Allocate weekly time to sales planning as well as doing sales / marketing.
- Think about how you could develop / redevelop your business to focus on a specific niche.
- Build some initial sales foundations as early as possible.
- Elevator pitches are incredibly important – work on them!
- Give time to developing and continually improving your sales foundations and service offering.
- Learn how the traditional sales process works.
- Learn how to network effectively and do so.
- Learn how to do social selling.

What Sales Planning Helps You Understand

Good sales planning should help you understand the answers to the following questions:

- What is the marketplace you are focusing on?
- Who is the competition in your sector?
- Who do you ideally want to be selling to?
- Who is your target audience?
- What are the pain points of your target audience?
- What is your niche?
- What is your product / service offering?
- How much does your product / service cost?
- What are the features of your product / service?
- What are the benefits of your product / service?
- What differentiates your product / service from the competition?
- What are the USPs of your product / service?
- Why are people likely to need your product / service?
- How are you going to pitch the product / service succinctly and effectively?
- What is your sales and marketing strategy?
- How will your target audience be able to find info on what you are selling?
- How will you get warm enquiries coming to you?
- Who will be selling for your business?
- What is your sales budget?
- What is your marketing budget?
- What is your digital development budget?
- What sales / marketing and digital materials do you plan to develop?
- What is your networking strategy?

Social media and other forms of digital marketing can be great and cost-effective ways for small businesses to promote themselves. However, if there is not a good sales strategy behind this activity, or if other areas of sales foundation work and sales and marketing planning are overlooked, then good results can be extremely slow in coming! This is one of the key reasons why sales planning is so important.

CHAPTER 4:

The Difference Between Sales and Marketing

Why is it So Difficult to Distinguish Between Sales and Marketing?

The simple answer is that the lines have become extremely blurred, so it can be difficult to tell the difference! Throw in more elements such as advertising, digital materials and social media, and it can become even more confusing.

One of the biggest problems with the fact that the lines between the two have got so blurry is that a lot of small businesses do marketing but forget to implement key sales elements. This is a major problem because without considering the sales elements and putting strong sales foundations in place, a lot of the time and money spent on marketing can be wasted.

Untangling Sales and Marketing

These days, sales and marketing are closely intertwined with a lot of similarities and crossover. So, for me to effectively explain the difference between sales and marketing we need to start by untangling them, and I think the best place to start is by explaining what my perception of sales is.

What Exactly is Sales?

What does the word 'sales' really mean?

As far as the B2B SME sector is concerned, I think it's relatively simple — I think it means the things you need to put in place / do to appeal to the right audience, gain quality enquiries and secure new clients, and sell products / services. Ultimately, it's about encouraging the right people to buy what you have for sale.

I often wonder why so many SMEs put so much time into marketing (predominantly social media) yet seem to forget the importance of sales in the term 'sales and marketing'. I regularly look around me at the marketing activity small businesses are doing, and I see their lack of sales focus and I just think to myself, why?

- Why are they wasting time and money on marketing when the sales basics are not right?
- Why do they keep doing the same things which are highly unlikely to be working effectively because the sales basics are not right?
- Why don't they do something to improve the sales basics?
- Why don't they learn how to sell?

It also astounds me that many small business owners don't like the word 'sales'. It's almost as if it is a dirty word.

If you say the word 'sales' to some small business owners, you can almost see them shudder as it generates the idea of used car sales dealers or unscrupulous door-to-door salespeople.

The Fear of Cold-calling

I assume in their minds it conjures up images of seeing themselves having to knock on doors or do other forms of cold-calling which they find so distasteful that they avoid sales at all costs. This means avoiding specialists who might teach them how to gain new clients too (oh, the irony).

It's a misconception that I think causes so many problems – especially as the specialists these small business owners do seem to turn to are often the ones offering free or cheap services about social media on social media that provide very little value. Often because these specialists have limited experience or expertise in sales themselves.

The type of cold-calling that evokes such distasteful images and disdain from going anywhere near anything to do with the word 'sales' isn't even the type of sales small businesses need to do these days. And anyway, even when you did have to do 'cold-calling' in a professional B2B environment, it was never so unsavoury.

In my experience, cold-calling in a professional B2B environment years ago was all about finding good leads (prospects) and about slowly but surely building up a relationship and getting people to know, like and trust you (generally via telesales).

Sales does still require an element of cold-calling but now the initial 'cold-calling' (as it were) just tends to happen in a different way – through first-time meetings / intros at networking events (online and offline), local events, social selling etc.

You could potentially still do telesales too, but there are legalities to be aware of with this, and good telesales activity takes good training – again, it's an area I would suggest talking to specialists about if you want to do this, so you ensure you do it well and within the necessary guidelines.

Personally, I think there is so much opportunity with networking, social selling and events etc. that I don't think telesales work is needed these days for most small businesses.

Why You Should Embrace Sales

The problems so many small business owners seem to have is they either don't understand the word 'sales' and what it means, or they fear it due to the misconception they have of it in their minds. Another reason is they don't know how to sell and / or they lack confidence. Whatever the reason, as a result, they steer away from sales and just veer into marketing. This is such a big and unnecessary mistake.

Small business owners really do need to realise that sales is not something to shy away from or be fearful of, as without a continual flow of sales your business could sadly become one of the many that do not make it.

My summary of the relationship between sales and marketing is below.

> Sales is what drives revenue and revenue is what drives business growth – the two are interlinked, and marketing is primarily just a conduit to raise brand awareness and help make sales. Without the need for sales, marketing would be somewhat redundant.

If you want to gain new business on an ongoing basis, then stop for a moment and think about the paragraph on the previous page and what the term 'sales' really means to you and your business. Ask yourself why it is so important and how getting the sales side right could enhance the social media, marketing and other promotional activity you are doing.

Remember my definition of sales – I define it as the things you need to put in place or do to appeal to the right audience, gain quality enquiries, secure new clients, and sell products / services. Ultimately, it's about encouraging the right people to buy what you have for sale.

Some of the things I think small businesses should do on the sales side before putting too much into marketing efforts are below.

- Assess your sales foundations.
- Look at your target market from a sales perspective.
- Think about the niche(s) in which you wish to operate / focus.
- Work out your USPs and tagline etc.
- Decide on your service offering and pricing, and create some packages.
- Ensure you have a good sales strategy – which takes good sales planning.
- Learn about the traditional sales process and how to sell.
- Start thinking about sales as much as (if not more than) marketing.
- Start embracing sales instead of overlooking it or shying away from it.

I firmly believe sales should be considered as important as marketing (if not more important). As far as most small business owners are concerned, I think sales should come before marketing!

Ideally, the two need to work in conjunction with one another but the development of strong sales foundations and a sales planning strategy should, in my view, always come first. Yet from everything I see, read and hear, many small business owners totally overlook much of what I've mentioned.

The Pillars of Promotion

Sales. I have provided an overview of sales on the previous pages and, to summarise, I define it as the things you need to put in place / do to appeal to the right audience, gain quality enquiries, secure new clients and sell products / services. Ultimately, it's about encouraging the right people to buy what you have for sale.

Marketing is essentially how you promote your product or service and sales messages (directly or indirectly) via different distribution methods (e.g. social media, podcasts, newsletters). It includes the messaging / content you use, which can overlap with sales. This is one example of those blurry lines between the two, as marketing material often contains sales messages!

Branding, public relations (PR) and SEO all come under the general marketing umbrella. However, these services are also totally independent areas, each one with its own complexities and benefits.

- Targeted / niche marketing is about finding ways to get in front of a specific audience and deliver your sales and marketing messages effectively.
- Local marketing is as the name suggests – marketing to a local audience. Typical forms of local marketing include social media marketing, local search, local PR, segmented email marketing, and more traditional marketing like direct mail and event marketing. Local networking could also be

included here, as networking is a form of promotion that is a cross between sales and marketing.

- Account-based marketing refers to being extremely strategic in who you approach with a quality over quantity focus. In my mind, this is essentially sales work and not really marketing at all. It's been named marketing though, and now sits under the marketing umbrella, which just adds to the confusion.

Aside from social media (and particularly social selling), the three types of marketing mentioned above and on the previous page are probably the best and most cost-effective ways to market effectively at the outset for the type of businesses this book is aimed at.

Advertising. Most marketing is paid for in one way or another, even if not directly. For example, time spent on social media activity has a cost, as time equates to money. However, some forms of marketing are paid for directly, such as PPC (pay per click search on major search engines) and social media paid ads, so this type of marketing really should be classed as advertising. I class 'advertising' as any form of promotional activity where you pay directly for visitors or page views, or pay an upfront flat-rate fee. There are numerous forms of paid advertising, such as press ads, radio, TV, paid editorial (advertorial), outdoor advertising paid ads, PPC (pay per click – or paid search) and paid social media advertising. Please note, that whilst PPC is technically advertising, I also reference it throughout the book as a form of inbound marketing, which it is often seen as.

Digital and offline materials is the term I use to describe things you use to deliver your message (whether aligned to sales, marketing, advertising or all of these). So, this would include your website, social media pages, sales materials (e.g. PDFs) and promotional material.

These materials all form part of the strong sales foundations that I think need to be built before you start spending too much time and / or money on marketing and other promotional activity.

Knowing what falls under sales and what's marketing can be so confusing as there is a lot of crossover. This said, it can be broken down to a degree as I have outlined.

Social Media

One of the reasons it has become so confusing is because **social media** crosses all four areas I've outlined (i.e. sales, marketing, advertising and digital materials) and it can be used in several ways, as shown below.

- Social selling (aligned to sales) – This is where you use social media channels to network online and communicate with connections and prospects (by commenting and direct messaging etc.) with a view to building rapport and sales opportunity. The objective is to take the relationship elsewhere at the point when it's felt by both sides that the conversation needs to become more detailed. This could start with email communication, or it could involve a video call, a phone call, or a face-to-face meeting. By taking the conversation elsewhere it then continues along the traditional sales process trajectory.
- Social media marketing (aligned to marketing) – This is where you use social media to promote your marketing material – usually done by the creation of different types of social media posts. There are several types of post – text post, carousel, polls etc. and there are all sorts of other ways to market your business on social media too, including audio sessions, video etc.

- Social page creation (aligned to digital materials) – This could be personal pages and business pages on social channels.
- Social media ads (aligned to advertising) – This is where you pay the social media channels (usually a price per click) to run advertising campaigns. There are various types of social media advertising opportunities. These can sometimes be a lot cheaper than SEO or PPC, so if sales foundations are built well, they can potentially be a good option (if planned and managed well).

One important thing to note with any social media activity, is that if other elements of work relating to sales, such as building strong sales foundations and sales planning are not done well, then social media activity is likely to be far less effective than it could be.

This can make social media activity time-consuming for a low return. This is one of the key reasons small businesses can waste time and money on social media and it relates to the leaky bucket scenario outlined on page 14 and 15.

Having a very good website with great content and sales messaging can enhance social media activity greatly.

Also, if the time you are dedicating to social media is clearly raising brand awareness and getting lots of impressions, but you are still not getting enough interactions or enquiries or making sales, it could be that your sales and / or marketing messaging needs improving. Or it may be because you don't have strong sales foundations in place and you're experiencing a severe case of leaky bucket syndrome.

There is no point pouring more and more liquid into the social media marketing bucket if it has holes in the bottom! You need to glue up the holes first and that takes good sales planning.

So, I have now explained the five areas associated with the term 'sales and marketing' — relisted below:

- Sales
- Marketing
- Advertising & PR / paid promotion
- Digital materials
- Social media.

There is also one more to add to the above, which although it falls under marketing should for the purpose of this book be dealt with separately, and that is SEO (search engine optimisation). The reason I want to deal with this separately is because it is a complex area, but one that holds a lot of opportunity, sales-wise, for SMEs. I will explain this in much more detail in Chapter 19 which is all about SEO and how it influences and impacts sales.

A Summary of the Differences Between Sales and Marketing

Let's summarise the differences between the two core terms — sales and marketing.

Sales relates to the things you need to put in place or do to appeal to the right audience, gain quality enquiries, secure new clients, and sell products / services. Ultimately, it's about encouraging the right people to buy what you have for sale.

To do this effectively you must have strong sales foundations, a good sales planning strategy and know how to sell.

If you don't know how to sell, then it's probably a good idea to do a short course locally, or at least attend workshops or do some online learning around this subject.

Marketing is not generally about communicating directly with individual prospects, but instead it's about getting your brand messages in front of a wider audience. Ideally, this should be a highly targeted audience, though this isn't always possible.

Marketing is also about testing different ways to get in front of users, deliver sales and marketing messages, and encourage visitors to see your brand / digital materials (e.g. your website).

Marketing should also involve things such as marketplace analysis, monitoring activity and response rates, and acting on the results of findings – i.e. adapting your marketing to do more of the things that work well and less of the activity that doesn't produce results.

Crossover Between Sales and Marketing

There are various areas in which sales and marketing overlap because the two disciplines are so closely aligned these days. These include some of the things that I class as foundational sales work such as competitor analysis, SWOT analysis, establishing your target audience, website planning, SEO planning and copywriting.

These days it's almost impossible to decipher what falls under sales and what is marketing with many of these core fundamental elements. For the purpose of this book, I class this fundamental work as part of the sales planning process, as it runs alongside building strong sales foundations in the 10-point UniC sales planning process.

I feel there is good reason to class it as 'sales work' too, as it aligns to the type of work I was always taught to do by sales managers and trainers in various sales roles in a long-standing sales career. The difference is that some of this work now needs to be adapted to work with digital and this has meant there needs to be a few adaptions and additions such as website planning and SEO planning.

The foundation work for sales activity should always be done before marketing! If it isn't, then as I've said before, your marketing activity will be like trying to fill a bucket with liquid when the bucket is full of holes.

How Are Sales Made?

Sales can be made by hunting for the sales prospects and delivering good sales messaging through highly targeted sales activity, marketing, networking, social selling and one-to-one meetings.

Before you start trying to make more sales it's important to note that the following seven things can all play a big part in helping you make more sales.

- Strong sales foundations
- Sales planning
- A great sales strategy
- Knowing steps of the traditional sales process
- Learning how to network effectively
- Learning how to sell
- Gaining a good understanding of social selling.

To sell effectively you are highly likely to need to do the following once you have done initial sales planning and identified your target market and niche.

- Get in front of the right target audience (or get them to come to you).
- Create the right sales messaging to entice leads – e.g. good elevator pitches, website copy and social media pages.

- Hold sales meetings – online (video) or offline (face-to-face).
- Ask questions.
- Listen to answers.
- Define the prospect's needs through effective questioning.
- Relay the features, benefits and USPs of your product or service.
- Match benefits to client needs.
- Identify buying signals.
- Answer client's questions effectively.
- Overcome concerns (handle objections).
- Close the sale – whilst online activity can be a great way to generate good enquiries, I believe closing sales still very often requires a face-to-face meeting or at least a phone or video call.

The above points, which all relate to the traditional sales process, are discussed in more depth in Chapter 6.

To create methods to entice your target audience to find you and produce incoming sales enquiries, you'll need to do activity such as local search, SEO, PPC, social media or advertising, and then send them through a digital sales funnel.

How the many elements of the traditional sales process translate to online sales will be explained in Chapter 7 but, as a summary, how the digital sales element of things work online is outlined below and on the next page.

A Summary of the Digital Sales Process

When using methods of inbound marketing (such as SEO, PPC, and content marketing) to drive traffic to your website, most visitors should be the right type of visitors because they will have found your website through highly targeted methods – i.e. by searching for keywords on search engines, or seeing useful content.

When these good-quality prospects arrive at your digital door (essentially your website, landing pages and / or social media page), the sales messaging and sales funnel / sales signage must be good enough to turn a good percentage of visitors into enquiries. You then need to convert these enquiries into conversations and ideally one-to-one meetings where you can use traditional sales skills to close sales.

This is one of the key reasons why a website is so important as part of the digital sales process. It acts as an amazing sales brochure and, to a degree, can essentially be viewed as the online salesperson.

It's there to direct visitors through the site via good content and frequently asked questions so that as many visitors as possible pass neatly through this sales tool and to the contact form and / or enquiry page. Once they have done this, you can then arrange sales calls and / or meetings.

This is where good use of social media can be a very cost-effective way of generating sales enquiries initially, as if the other key elements (e.g. landing pages, website) are developed well, social media can be a free method that drives traffic (visitors). It still requires good sales-focused strategic planning to work effectively though.

Good social media pages can do a similar thing as a website (in terms of acting as a sales funnel, but only from visitors that find you on the social platform – not generally from other methods) – whereas a website sits centrally to most forms of promotion /

marketing and therefore visitors can find a website in all sorts of ways, including from social media.

Social media can however be used as a very useful free method to drive traffic to a website. So, a good social media strategy can be incredibly valuable for digital sales once everything else is in place.

An Overview of Branding

Branding is one area that I have not mentioned yet that I firmly believe needs to be planned at the same time as sales planning. My definition of 'branding' is creating a strong and memorable identity and image for your business (or product / service).

Some people might think that branding should be done before sales planning but given how important developing a strong brand is for SMEs in relation to the sales process (digital in particular), I think this is an outdated perception. I believe it is incredibly important that branding (or rebranding, as is often required) is done in line with sales planning.

Just ask yourself these questions if you don't agree with me.

- How can SMEs develop a strong brand to attract and appeal to their target audience if they haven't worked out who this audience is from a sales perspective?
- How can a brand be positioned effectively to drive sales enquiries if you haven't quite worked out what you're selling?
- How can the hub of your business – i.e. your website – be positioned to make a great first impression as a brand if you haven't worked out what your brand values are in alignment with your sales purpose?

As far as I am concerned, branding and the early stages of sales planning need to be considered in unison.

Rebranding and / or Repositioning

So, what if you already have a brand but have not yet started sales planning?

The answer is 'don't worry'.

If you already have a brand and don't want to change your brand name, there are various ways to rebrand or reposition your brand when you do start to do sales planning. This is one of the areas where specialist help can be invaluable.

Sometimes you can totally change your brand name if you want. However, changing an existing brand name is not always advisable as it can cause many administration issues, digital issues, and, potentially, legal issues. So, specialist advice should be sought before doing this.

Also, you must be very careful if you are already generating traffic from SEO, as by changing a domain name you could lose SEO visitors if this is not dealt with professionally. I would always recommend seeking the advice of an SEO agency if you have existing search traffic but want to change your brand and domain name, or if you want to change URLs or pages on the site as part of the rebrand.

Branding overlaps with sales and marketing in areas such as web development, content writing and messaging, so as the sales planning process takes shape and progresses, this should be done in conjunction with branding and brand planning.

First impressions count for so much, and when running a small business, the branding, sales and marketing processes need to work together and have cross-channel consistency and continuity to be most effective. There needs to be a professional and cohesive approach. To achieve this, I see the 'brand' like a fine chain that runs through every aspect of sales and marketing, seamlessly holding it together.

Foundational Sales Problems

Many small business owners find it hard to differentiate between sales and marketing, and also branding.

They often overlook lots of important elements of the digital development side too which can be very problematic as it is important for sales. Some of the key issues I see business owners come up against in the SME market that relate to foundational sales elements are listed below.

- They overlook the importance of having a strong brand
- They overlook building strong sales foundations
- They often spend too much time doing social media badly
- They waste their time doing digital activity when a well-thought-out strategic, targeted and hybrid approach is likely to be far more effective in terms of delivering early sales
- They don't assign a big enough marketing budget to branding or digital development
- They totally underestimate the value of a website
- They become disheartened with digital and pull budget too soon
- They don't take a cohesive approach
- They don't think about (and plan for) inbound marketing soon enough.

Problems Caused by Not Having Strong Sales Foundations

Whilst most SMEs are usually active on social media, and often trial other areas of digital marketing like SEO, they can find it hard to gain traction and make sales! When they eventually realise that they've wasted a lot of time and / or money on digital activity that hasn't achieved good results, they become disenchanted with digital. This often leads to a downward spiral where the business owner feels cheated and disheartened, and loses all belief in sales and marketing, and pulls the budget.

With this last point, the problem is an obvious one to me and it's not that digital does not work. The issue is that the business owner tries hard with what they perceive to be the right digital activity, but, unfortunately, they either do the wrong activity or they do the right activity but badly.

Often, the biggest problem is that they totally fail to build strong sales foundations (including digital development elements such as a website). They also don't do enough (if any) sales planning, so they are continually going through the marketing mangle, trying to fill a hole-ridden bucket.

Another big issue is that SMEs often confuse social media activity to essentially be digital marketing, when in fact it is just one small element of digital marketing. There are a multitude of marketing and promotional options, and the best approach is to be strategic with promotional activity and plan it in conjunction with sales activity. Also, if social media is the only form of digital marketing that is being used, then it needs to be used well with a good strategy in line with well-thought-out sales planning and strong sales foundations. Without these things, social media activity is likely to be time-consuming with poor results.

Three More Typical Sales-related Mistakes SMEs Make

I think small business owners often make three other major mistakes in the early years that could be easily rectified if things were planned properly, sales-wise, from the outset.

- They fail to plan / develop a good-quality website early on
- If they do build a good website, they often fail to build it with strong SEO foundations
- They spend too much time doing social media marketing when social selling could potentially be a much better option.

The bottom line is that quality incoming enquiries and / or sales won't just appear! A salesperson (possibly the business owner) needs to take a proactive approach using more traditional sales methods online and offline – which is the approach outlined in the 10-point UniC sales planning process. Alternatively, a digital strategy needs to be planned, developed and continually worked on. In an ideal world, I think it should be a combination of both things.

However, on the digital side, if there is not enough targeted traffic, sales will not be made. If no salesperson is doing the selling, then digital sales elements (i.e. strong sales foundations such as a good website) must be in place to replace the salesperson. If sales foundations are not strong, then potential sales simply will be lost time and again!

When things aren't working on the digital and / or sales side, SMEs usually don't understand why. They seem to think that because they are doing lots of social media activity, or because they tried SEO (for example) for a few months, they should just get results (enquiries and sales). When the results don't emerge, it can be extremely disappointing! This can have a negative effect for the business.

If the business owner does not realise why things are not working and thinks they can't improve things, this is the point that they can lose faith. This can result in them stopping putting budget and / or time into sales and marketing.

When this happens, it puts the business in a very precarious position, as starving a business of future sales is like removing the oxygen a business needs to breathe. Without a pipeline of sales, most businesses will ultimately collapse.

The 10-point UniC sales planning process should help SMEs avoid these foundational and fundamental sales problems and provide a roadmap for SMEs to do sales planning effectively.

CHAPTER 5:

Why Sales Before Marketing

The lines between sales and marketing have become extremely blurred in recent years and there is a lot of crossover between the two disciplines. However, it's very important for small businesses to understand the differences between the two, as generating sales is what ultimately leads to business success.

In this book I want to explain why it's so important to put sales before marketing and how to do this effectively for low cost. Sales propel a business forward, and good sales results underpin business success, so I'm surprised at how many small business owners don't consider the fundamentals of sales or focus more heavily on sales planning.

Why So Many SMEs Miss Out the Sales Piece of the Jigsaw

I think so many SMEs overlook sales planning and focus primarily on marketing for seven main reasons.

- Because they don't realise the importance of sales planning
- Digital development can be complex, costly and confusing, and because digital now plays an integral role in sales, people are confused by the whole thing. Or they don't initially have budget to invest in this
- They think they have sales covered because they find it difficult to differentiate between sales and marketing
- Or they think you don't need to differentiate as they think sales and marketing are one and the same thing – which they are not!
- They receive poor advice from people claiming to be specialists who don't have the experience, expertise or knowledge to provide good enough strategic input
- They don't have experience in sales and / or marketing, but they don't put enough emphasis on working with specialists and instead try and go it alone
- They fear the word 'sales' for whatever reason and shy away from learning about sales or doing sales activity.

Experience tells me that if you were to ask 100 small business owners how many of them spend time on sales planning or building sales foundations, a high percentage would say they don't. But I think many will be likely to think they don't need to because, for some reason, they'll be under the misapprehension that this is covered by their marketing activity.

Some Points Regarding Sales and Marketing

The points on the following two pages are worth thinking about and remembering when you want to gain new clients as they act as a reminder of why the 10-point UniC sales planning process is so important.

Q: Can you make sales without marketing?

A: Yes.

Q: Can you make sales without sales planning?

A: Yes – but you could easily make a lot more with good sales planning.

Q: Can you undertake marketing activity without sales planning?

A: Yes, but results from this activity are likely to be poor – this is because it will be like trying to fill a bucket that has holes in the bottom. The marketing budget will leak out and be wasted by watering weeds instead of the sales seeds.

Q: Do you need a professionally built website to make sales?

A: No, but a good website should become your best tool to assist in the sales and marketing process because it sits centrally to most other forms of sales and promotional activity. It can act like an online brochure and to a degree an online salesperson. The sooner you have a professionally built website, the better it will be for your sales and marketing activity.

Q: Why don't many marketing specialists tell SMEs to do sales planning?

A: I think there are four primary reasons for this:

- Because the lines are so blurred. If marketing specialists are not sales specialists themselves, they do not always recognise the importance of building strong sales foundations.
- Or they may consider sales and marketing to be one and the same thing (which they're not!) and as such they may think they cover all the necessary sales elements with what they do. But if they're not trained in sales and / or if they don't have in-depth understanding of web development and inbound marketing, it's highly unlikely they will cover sales elements effectively.
- Marketing specialists might think the sales process comes after marketing. In my view, this is totally incorrect. Whilst an element of sales activity may come after marketing (e.g. liaising with enquirers, handling objections and closing), I firmly believe building strong sales foundations (both online and offline) and sales planning should always come before marketing!
- Many marketers monitor the wrong metrics and think they are doing a good job, even though the ROI is poor due to a lack of sales planning. They spend too much time focusing on vanity metrics like visitor numbers as opposed to the metrics that really count – the metrics that monitor interactions. These relate to sales and can be all sorts of things from clicks around a site to multiple pages, newsletter sign-ups, contact form enquiries, PDF downloads, comments and direct contact. Essentially, anything that shows real interest and allows you to begin direct communication with a prospect.

CHAPTER 6:

The Traditional Sales Process

Many salespeople that work for big companies are often sent on intensive sales training courses. This is because there is a process to traditional sales that can be taught and learnt.

By traditional sales, I mean when people are selling to others using traditional methods (i.e. not digital methods) – face-to-face and via the telephone being two of the originals. These days there are other ways, but some of these take place digitally such as online networking, social selling, video calls – essentially any method that allows one-to-one direct communication whether it be online or offline.

From what I see, whilst many small business owners are the primary salesperson for their business, very few of them seem to be trained in the traditional sales process and a lot of them don't seem to make use of the many direct sales methods that are freely available to them.

I am of a very strong opinion that for most small business owners the best way to make sales early on is by building strong sales foundations and undertaking sales planning. Then following the key steps of the traditional sales process using both online and offline methods. This is what I refer to as a hybrid approach.

It is a particularly good way to progress if the marketing budget available is low. This is because more emphasis can be put on low-cost and free methods of promotional activity early on as these are likely to prove to be far more successful if sales foundations and sales planning have been done well.

Why Traditional Sales Activity is So Important

Highly targeted forms of digital marketing such as SEO and PPC are a fantastic way to generate warm incoming sales enquiries, but these forms of marketing activity generally take money to be successful. For SEO, for example, a monthly budget of £500+ is a low-entry point and it can be much more depending how much work you want done.

Most small business owners with low marketing budgets don't have the resources to invest in this type of inbound marketing on an ongoing basis to begin with. Therefore, traditional sales-based activity is probably one of the most cost-effective and fast turnaround methods to make sales.

One thing I would say is that I believe that results from 'social selling' activity can enhance traditional sales activity greatly. So, my recommendation to most small businesses is to combine traditional sales activity / networking with social selling initially, alongside low-cost promotional activity like local events.

I also think general social media can be a great way to generate interest when done strategically in line with the creation of strong sales foundations and good sales planning. However, you usually need to take enquiries from social media to offline communication and into a typical traditional sales process to convert these types of enquiries into warm prospects (i.e. people who are close to making a decision / or in buying mode).

To undertake any sales activity successfully you require strong sales foundations (as outlined in Chapter 3) and a good sales strategy (as outlined in Chapter 7). However, you also need to have a good understanding of the traditional sales process and know how to use this effectively.

Breakdown of Key Elements of the Traditional Sales Process

Making sales involves a tried-and-tested process that enables you to identify the right prospects, understand their needs, explain the features of your product / service, promote the benefits of the product / service and match these benefits to the needs of the client, handle objections, and close the sale.

To do this effectively both through traditional sales methods and digital sales you need to do the following:

- Understand your target audience, know where to find them, and have a strategy to either get in front of them, or get them to come to you so you can deliver your sales message.
- Know your competition and what differentiates you from them.
- Know your USPs – unique selling points (of your company and products / services).
- Have a clear idea of what you are selling – i.e. a very good understanding of your product / service range.

- Know the strengths and weaknesses of your business.
- Know the features of your products / services – what are the key points about them and what do they do?
- Know the benefits of your products / services – how do the key points and what they do benefit your target audience / prospects?
- Use questioning techniques to establish needs and listen to answers.
- Throughout the questioning process use a lot of open questions – what, when, why, where, who, how. These types of questions require an answer and not just a 'Yes' or 'No' – and encourage interaction and open discussion.
- Listen to answers and ask more questions accordingly.
- Position the features, benefits and USPs of your product and / or service effectively with good messaging – this can be done most effectively by direct communication and creating a good website and social media landing pages etc.
- Pitch your product and service effectively – these days, this requires an understanding of traditional and digital sales processes. It also usually requires elevator pitches for use online and / or offline.
- Recognise buying signals.
- Encourage communication to highlight issues / problem areas and overcome concerns / objections.
- Use closing techniques and have some form of mechanism to finalise a sale.

To position and pitch your product / service effectively requires many things on the sales planning side, such as branding work, competitor analysis, target market research, USP (unique selling point) work, service creation, and pricing.

All of the above points are explained in much more detail in Part 2 of the book.

To sell effectively in the traditional way (i.e. face-to-face or by verbal communication) you need to undertake some form of sales activity (e.g. networking, meetings, pitches, presentations). This can take place online (e.g. social selling and online networking / meetings) or offline (networking and sales meetings / presentations).

Key Requirements for Effective Sales / Small Business Growth

- Objectives
  - In terms of what you want to achieve as a business
  - Financial
  - Sales-focused
  - Digital growth-focused.
- You need to have confidence in what you are selling.
- You need to make a very good first impression both offline and online.
- You need to understand the key points relating to your target audience.
- You need to be able to easily get in front of the target audience as often as possible, via online and / or offline methods.
- You need strong messaging that quickly delivers your message to the target audience.
- You need your brand to stand out from the crowd and make people choose you over the competition.
- You need good USPs and key selling points that can be quickly relayed via elevator pitches.
- You need to be responsive (quick) in terms of providing additional sales info to any warm leads you get.
- You need to manage your time carefully and / or outsource sales / marketing / digital activity, as sales will not come without time being put in one way or another.

- If you want to gain incoming leads, then you need to devise and implement an 'inbound marketing' strategy which needs to be aligned to sales planning strategy.
- For SMEs, I believe it's incredibly important to know how to network effectively and sell well, face-to-face. Training may be required as this can make it so much more effective.
- You need a sales plan.
- You need to continually build a sales pipeline.
- You need to have an understanding of social selling.

Key Considerations Before You Start to Sell

- Decide upon brand values and create a strong brand.
- Know exactly what you are selling – what are your products / services and what price are you selling them at.
- Know who exactly you want to sell to – it doesn't have to be just one group but you must have a clear idea of who your target market is.
- Know what makes you different and better than your competition – this will require some competitor analysis.
- Know in-depth information about all the key features of your service or product offering.
- Know what specific benefits your product or service hold for your customer.
- Get your messaging right – online and offline – which will incorporate all sorts of things from USPs to values etc.
- Ensure all the fundamental sales elements are in place – branding, good website, key social pages, sales literature.
- Plan how you are going to sell.
- Get in front of the right target audience as often as possible – either by putting yourself in front of them via networking, workshops, direct sales, social selling etc., or getting them to come to you – this can take many forms, such as social media marketing and inbound marketing (e.g. SEO, PPC, digital PR).

- You'll need to build and nurture a prospect list and communicate with potential prospects in various ways.
- Build and nurture relationships with your potential referrers (your network).
- Have all the tools ready to be responsive to warm leads / enquiries and quickly provide good info to warm leads.
- Do a good job – i.e. provide a quality service.
- Provide great customer care.
- Get good feedback and recommendations / testimonials from clients.
- Spread the word of the good feedback and encourage others to spread the word too.
- Nurture the relationship with existing clients and upsell.
- Build your brand awareness – thought-leadership pieces etc.
- Make sure you have all the legalities in place to sell effectively – e.g. contracts, privacy policies, IT security. It's important to speak to specialists about all these areas.

The Art of a Good Salesperson

To me, sales is second nature. I went into sales so young; I had a natural aptitude for it, and I was so well trained for the early part of my career that my sales skill has essentially become a part of my personality.

What differentiates my style of selling, from salespeople that are not so competent, is that when I'm networking, I can work a room and make sales progress, without people feeling they are being sold to. I am genuinely interested in people too and happy to listen to their stories, and these things help get me good leads.

When selling, I take a consultancy-style approach. This means I am willing to take things slowly and be helpful and generous with my time and expertise. I expect to have lots of interactions before a sale is made and I am always prepared to walk away. I never expect to sell there and then, and I believe that this helps immensely.

I think if you are genuinely prepared to walk away that people sense you are not desperate to sell – this makes the sales process easier. I don't know the ins and outs of the psychology behind it – other sales books will probably explain that. What I do know is that it is something I was taught to do and something that has undoubtedly worked well for me.

I realise sales is a long game and I also realise that if I don't sell but I do communicate well, then a meeting may still result in a referral, a recommendation or word spreading about the service I provide. These are all things that could help future sales.

This consultancy approach I take puts potential prospects at ease; it makes them comfortable enough to talk. It allows me to listen and ask lots of questions, and it builds rapport and earns trust.

When networking or selling, I also smile and dress well, as first impressions count! My body language is good, I listen, I ask the right questions, I listen again, I provide the right answers. I don't rush or push people into anything (or at least they don't feel that way) and I simply build business relationships and keep the relationship going after the initial meeting by following up relatively quickly. So, I nurture my leads well too.

I plan things well and I am usually very ahead of the game in terms of booking networking events and managing my diary and client meetings. So, I don't miss out on good sales opportunities. One thing I teach the clients I work with is how important it is to be organised and manage your time effectively when selling – especially if you are the lone (or primary) salesperson for a business.

In addition, I keep going where others would often give up. Many sales specialists say it takes numerous interactions before a sale is made (7+) but this is something a lot of small businesspeople trying to make sales either do not realise or do not accept. So, they often give up too soon.

Lastly, I know how to spot buying signals, handle objections and close sales, and I have all the foundational sales work and sales planning in place to enable me to do this effectively (i.e. I have the right tools for the job, such as a sales toolkit, which I talk about in more detail in Chapter 14).

Key Things to Remember When Trying to Sell

There are a few things I think you must acknowledge if you want to be successful with sales.

- It's a numbers game.
- It's hard and full of rejections and you must be able to overcome this.
- You need to believe in the product / service you are selling and be able to convey the benefits of this quickly and effectively.
- You need to build a strong rapport and trust with potential prospects.
- You must be prepared to walk away – no-one likes a desperate / pushy salesperson.
- Sales always take longer to come in than you expect – prepare for this.

Points five and six are very important – never appear to be desperate or pushy in sales. People sense desperation, which puts them off, and people do NOT like pushy! So, when planning your business and / or building your sales pipeline, be prepared that sales are likely to take months to come in, not weeks (from the initial point of contact). If you are aware of this, and account for it from the outset, it should alleviate the need to be pushy.

Many sales trainers may not teach point 5 but I believe this is one of the keys to my sales success. If you are genuinely prepared to walk away, people sense it and it puts them at ease. This in turn makes the sales more likely. You can't fake it though. You must be prepared to walk.

The way I sell has worked for me for 30 years and it is something that I'm sure will continue to work for as long as I do it. Why? Because I was so keen to learn when I was young. I did one thing that all good salespeople should do – I listened intently.

I listened hard to all the professional training that I received in those early years and that held me in good stead sales-wise for life. This is primarily because there is a method and structure to follow when selling, and by listening, I learnt this process well! I also learnt from my own mistakes, and I'm still prepared to learn, and I still continue to learn, as having this attitude has always paid off sales-wise.

It's the Basics That Really Count

If I had to name 10 things that have made me into an excellent salesperson, I would say the following:

- The ability to ask good open questions
- Listening skills
- Good elevator pitches and delivery
- Taking a quality over quantity approach
- Excellent networking skills
- Taking a consultancy approach to sales – the 'know, like and trust' method – slow but effective

- Continual building of a sales pipeline
- Never being scared to walk away
- Ability to handle objections – which ironically is often done by reverting to points 1 and 2
- Persistence and perseverance.

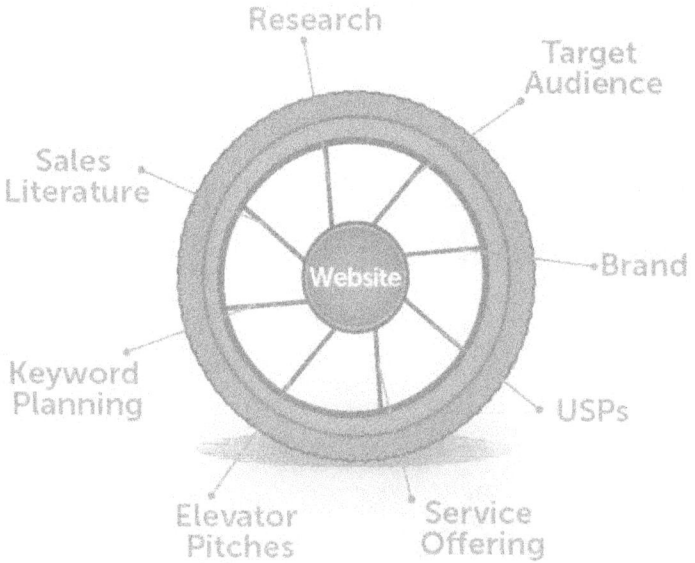

Research

Target Audience

Sales Literature

Website

Brand

Keyword Planning

USPs

Elevator Pitches

Service Offering

CHAPTER 7:

Aligning the Traditional Sales Process to Digital

A Definition of Digital Sales

These days, sales can be made solely by digital means, without any person-to-person interaction (i.e. via a website). However, strong sales foundations, good sales planning, excellent sales messaging and a sales process are all still required for this to be effective.

Throughout this book, when I refer to the term 'digital sales', it's best to assume that I use this to describe the sales elements of digital activity that help drive potential purchasers to make an enquiry. They might do this in various ways, such as by email, phone or a contact form.

With the type of service businesses (and high-value product businesses) I outlined at the beginning of the book, in my view, it's still best to go on to handle these enquiries with some form of human interaction once received. This could be via phone or tailored email communication, though ideally it would be via video meetings or, even better, a face-to-face meeting.

Smaller sales can, of course, be made purely by digital means, but I think higher-value sales of circa £200+ usually require the human touch.

Time will tell if I am wrong as things become even more digitised. However, I don't think I am wrong when it comes to small business sales. The digital marketplace has become too busy and too noisy, and therefore not responsive enough (in terms of answering bespoke questions, providing tailored packages etc.).

People like to buy from people – those they know, like and trust. This firm belief is one of the main reasons I think a hybrid approach to sales is the way forward for most B2B SMEs. In addition, digital sales without human interaction are far more likely to be made if you have a relatively high budget to invest in good digital marketing activity. But most SMEs don't have this level of budget initially, which makes interaction with people even more important.

Making Digital Sales

With digital sales, I believe the same rules apply as traditional sales. However, with digital you need to find a way to get your sales messages in front of enough potential clients. This is hard!

You also need to take most of the key elements from the traditional sales process and find a way to transfer this to digital. Then, you need to deliver the sales messages you want to your target audience without speech or human interaction in the first instance. That's incredibly difficult!

Once you have delivered a sales message good enough to entice an enquiry to be made, you can move the conversation offline and take the enquirer through the traditional sales process. Doing this can be challenging too.

In my opinion, the way for SMEs with low marketing budgets to have the best chance of achieving digital sales on an ongoing basis is usually through effective sales planning (including very good copywriting) AND combining this with highly targeted digital marketing.

This is why sales and marketing activity need to be very closely aligned when it comes to digital activity, which I'll explain in more detail later.

The first step to achieving high-quality enquiries via digital methods is to create very strong sales foundations. Once this is done, you still need to get your product / service seen by as many of the right people as possible. However, it essentially requires the reverse approach to traditional sales and that early door-knocking I did all those years ago.

A big element of digital sales is about bringing a highly targeted audience to your door as opposed to you knocking on theirs. This is what makes planning such an important part when it comes to digital sales.

Bringing Interested Visitors to Your Door

Bringing a highly targeted audience to your door usually means leading them to your website or social media pages. This can be done by various forms of well targeted marketing both offline and online.

The trick is that when they get to the door they are enticed to go in and have a look around, and this is where the sales element of digital activity really comes into play, and it's why having a good website and / or social media page(s) is so important.

Whilst marketing activity helps you get your sales messages in front of the right audience and lead prospects to your door, it's sales planning that helps plan who to target in the first place and what they see once they have reached your digital door(s).

It also helps direct them through the sales funnel (i.e. the rooms / pages behind the door) – a bit like wayfinding in the real world. Once they have been directed through a few pages it also helps lead them into another area where it converts them into enquiries and / or sales. The way to do this is through UX (user experience – including a good navigation system) and CRO (conversion rate optimisation) which means the text, graphics, buttons, videos etc. on the pages which have 'calls to action' – messages enticing visitors to click through to other pages.

Strong sales foundations can help turn quality sales prospects (or leads) into new conversions. Interested parties get converted into meetings or a request for a call etc. However, once the calls or meetings happen, things start to progress through the traditional sales process outlined in Chapter 6.

A well designed, professionally built website tends to help immensely with the digital sales process, and this is where branding, design, web development, content writing and potentially SEO can play a very positive part in helping to generate prospects and deliver sales.

Why a Website is Important

Your website is so important when it comes to positioning your business from a sales perspective. This will be explained in much more detail in Part 2 of the book but, for now, below are 10 reasons why your website is so important for sales.

- A website is one of the main 'sales' foundation stones.
- First impressions count for a lot when it comes to making sales.
- Your website sits centrally to most other forms of sales and marketing – pretty much all promotional routes lead to your website.
- Your website acts like a great brochure.
- Your business is likely to own your website – unlike social media pages.
- Content on your website can be used to drive visitors in several ways and content on your website can be evergreen with a long shelf life.
- Website content can easily be repurposed and used elsewhere.
- A good website forms the foundations required for SEO to be effective and other forms of inbound marketing to be effective. Get this working well and it is one of the best ways to drive warm (good quality) incoming enquiries.
- Your website address (domain name / brand name) is a great marketing tool as it can be promoted in a multitude of places.
- If it's planned and written well, in essence, your website can act like a salesperson for your business.

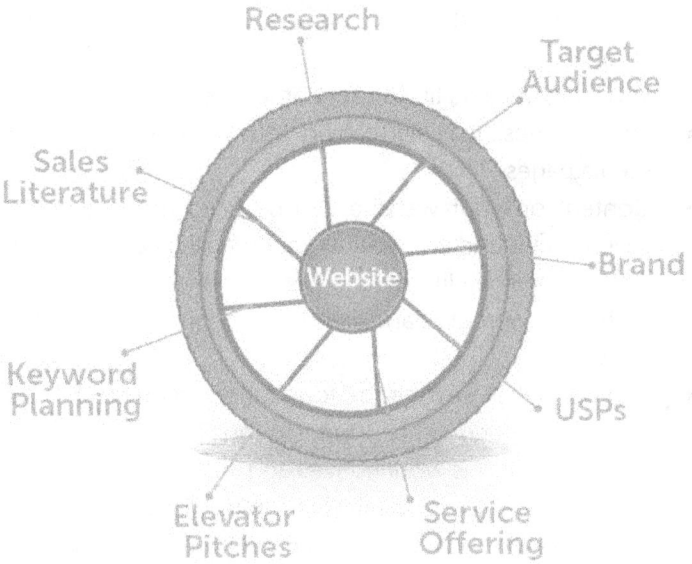

CHAPTER 8:

Why SEO Matters – Earlier Than You Think!

'Inbound marketing' is the term used to describe methods of marketing that produce visits to your website – i.e. incoming visits from people looking for your type of product or service, or interested in your content.

SEO (search engine optimisation) is one of the main methods of inbound marketing and is utilised to help your website achieve high listings on major search engines for keyword terms relevant to your business. These keyword terms will be the words and phrases your business' target audience will likely search for.

SEO continues to play a pivotal role in the digital sector. It is a very complex area though and to do SEO well requires many things to be considered and done, which is why it is usually best to work with an SEO specialist or agency.

My SEO specialism and experience covers keyword research and planning, website planning (SEO / content structure, plus information architecture [IA] and navigational elements), plus the writing of SEO-friendly content – all of which are closely aligned to sales. I also have a good understanding of all sorts of other elements of SEO, having worked with other SEO specialists for many years.

SEO (and other forms of inbound marketing) can be very beneficial for sales activity as it can drive highly targeted and warm leads, and these types of leads are often much easier to convert than leads generated by outreach or standard marketing activity.

This is because they are often people in buying mode because they have found your site when actively looking for terms related to your business

When it comes to making sales, having a good understanding of SEO and inbound marketing is advantageous for every SME.

Creating Strong SEO Foundations

Producing SEO-friendly content and applying ongoing SEO work can be extremely beneficial for long-term sales success, but this can be difficult for many SMEs to do in the early years due to cost.

However, it's a very good idea to think about SEO foundational work at the website-building stage. Even if monthly SEO work is not going to be undertaken at the outset (usually because costs are prohibitive), planning strong SEO foundations is something that should be considered at the sales planning stage.

Important Things to Note Regarding SEO

I will explain more about SEO and the important role it plays in sales in Chapter 19 but it's important to be aware of a few key points at this juncture.

- Keyword research is an integral part of both sales planning and SEO for several reasons.
- SEO work is something that sits centrally but spreads through and is impacted by all sorts of elements of sales, marketing and digital development.
- The foundational work for SEO is vitally important. This ideally needs to be done at the web development stage. This is because the website build is an integral part of SEO. Therefore, when spending money on having a professional website built it makes sense and is important to get the SEO foundations right at that point. This will hold you in good stead to apply further SEO in the future when you can afford it, even if it is not affordable to do this straight away.
- If you don't consider incorporating strong SEO foundations at the professional website build stage, then longer term, this may prove to be a costly mistake. This is because if you decide to start doing SEO further down the line you may have to spend more money redesigning the website, redeveloping the website, or even starting totally afresh with a new website because the SEO foundations have not been considered in the first place!

Incorporating SEO Foundational Work into Website Foundations

Think of a website like a tree, with the homepage as the trunk and all the top-level pages that lead from the trunk each being a main branch. From each main branch, smaller branches can grow.

So, for example, you could develop a website initially with 10 main pages leading from the homepage (these would be the main branches). Then, as time progresses, you could put links to two more pages (subsidiary branches) from each main page (branch) – other pages that lead from the main pages showing more of your services etc. – so your website grows to have 30 pages (and the homepage), just like a tree growing.

This will enable you to start building very well, from a general growth perspective, but also from an SEO and PPC perspective.

From an SEO perspective, if each page of the website that is built is planned with SEO in mind from the outset, and keyword research is done prior to the page build, then the site can be built so that it has strong SEO foundations with both the initial pages and the 20 new pages, plus it would be easy to develop more SEO-friendly pages the more the site grows.

If the SEO is not thought of at the beginning and applied badly to the first 30 pages in terms of planning, content and keyword usage etc. then it's easy to see why you may have to start from scratch again – as you may need to totally rewrite each page, replan the navigation system, do keyword research etc.

This is why it is so very important to think about keywords and SEO planning prior to building a good website – and not afterwards. From a digital development perspective, this is a very important thing to be aware of, and knowing this could save you both time and money in the future.

CHAPTER 9:

Putting It All Together: The UniC Sales Planning Process

As explained previously my expertise is very unusual because I have extensive experience of branding, sales, marketing, website planning, SEO, inbound marketing, content planning / copywriting, social selling and advertising.

This level of expertise and experience is unusually broad and over the past few years whilst working in the small business sector it has allowed me to take a bird's eye view of the challenges SMEs face in relation to making sales.

It has also allowed me to identify how SMEs could improve things by taking advantage of the low-cost opportunities available to them by adopting a far more strategic approach to sales.

I have translated this into my 10-point sales planning process which I have named 'the **UniC** sales planning process'. This is something that I believe small business owners can follow to achieve their own sales success.

The Basis of the 10-point UniC Sales Planning Process

If you think about it, a lot of small businesses have very small sales and marketing departments – it's often just the owner doing both things.

So, how do these owners / salespeople (or just one salesperson) get from A to B efficiently when there is so much to consider with sales and marketing?

The answer to this is that it's extremely difficult. That's why the 10-point UniC sales planning process incorporates a strong emphasis on each of the following things:

- Sales foundations
- Simplicity
- Structure
- Systematic methodology
- SEO (and other inbound marketing)
- Social selling
- Strategy.

Why Have I Named It 'The 10-point UniC Sales Planning Process'?

I think it is unique, and it is also a play on words that has been derived from the following analogy:

The Unicycle Analogy

When travelling by road, it is generally wheels that get you from A to B. Wheels are incredibly important – without them, very little progress would be made.

On the road there are all sorts of large and flash vehicles with wheels that could get you from A to B, including limousines, coaches and supercars. But you need to know how to drive these vehicles, how to handle them without crashing them, plus you need fuel to make them start and go anywhere. To go on a long journey, they need a lot of fuel. In this analogy, fuel equates to marketing budget.

However, you don't need a flash vehicle or a lot of fuel if you have an old-style, tried-and-tested method of transport – i.e. a unicycle.

One person could go a very long way with just one wheel and no fuel at all on a unicycle if the following 6 things applied:

- The wheel was strong.
- They knew where they were going and had a strategy to get there safely.
- They knew how to ride and keep good balance.
- They took regular breaks to rest, reassess the situation and recharge their energy.
- They had the resilience to pick themselves up and get back on each time they hit a hump in the road and had to get off (or worse still, were knocked off).
- They had a map to follow the best routes to achieve their goal.

As a small business owner, to make sales and achieve your sales objectives (reach the sales destination), you need the same tools and mindset as a unicycle rider – i.e. the tools required to get you to your desired destination, including a strong-enough wheel and the mechanism to make it turn, a good strategy to meet the objective, good balance and a route plan.

You also need the right mindset which, along with the strength and determination to complete the ride, requires you to acknowledge you need to take breaks and look after your wellbeing along the way.

Even if there is only one person in your business focused on sales initially, just like a unicycle rider, that one person can go a very long way with the right tools, strategy and mindset.

In this analogy, the following things apply:

- The wheel is the sales planning wheel.
- The sales planning wheel needs to be strong, like a unicycle wheel. This is what will get you from A to B. What makes up the wheel is explained further on.
- Having objectives of where you are going and following a good sales planning strategy to get there is another vital element.
- Keeping a good balance between various elements of sales and marketing is vital and this requires focus. To retain balance, a hybrid approach to sales and marketing is required (online and offline).
- A map, so you can plan routes at the outset and along the way. Sometimes the best routes only become clear as you start to progress.
- I'm a big believer in business owners / salespeople taking regular breaks and looking after their wellbeing. Sales can be stressful – everyone needs to rest and take time to reassess the situation and strategy. Much like with a unicycle rider, a far longer journey is likely to be achieved if these things are taken seriously and adhered to. Consultancy-style sales (the type of sales I would encourage) is not a speedy race – it's more like a long and slow journey, and to do well at it you

need to take care of yourself – that means taking breaks to recharge. As time progresses, sharing the cycling with other team members or outsourced helpers could also help spread the load.

- Picking yourself up and carrying on riding when selling gets hard, or when you take a business knock, will help immensely – I believe doing this is down to confidence, mindset and resilience.

There are a lot of similarities between a unicycle rider setting off to reach a destination, and a small business owner doing sales and marketing themselves and setting out to achieve sales success – so this analogy is what the word '**UniC**' in the 10-point sales planning process relates to.

Explanation of the UniC Sales Planning Wheel

The wheel in this analogy that I'm comparing to the unicycle wheel is the 'sales planning wheel'.

The sales planning wheel is essentially the visual representation of the 10-point UniC sales planning process as shown in Figure 1 on page 107.

Spokes – there are 8 spokes of the sales planning wheel which align to the 8 foundational elements in the sales planning process. These allow the wheel to function – the more of these that are missing, the weaker the wheel becomes.

The hub is the most central and pivotal point of the wheel and in essence the hub encapsulates all the things that make up the 'sales foundations'. This includes branding, sales messaging, sales information, USPs, features, benefits etc. and all the other things (listed on page 10) that are needed to create a strong brand with well-thought-out sales foundations. The spokes of the wheel (i.e. foundational elements) feed into the hub. The hub sits centrally and is the showcase / display case for all the foundational elements. In the real world, **the website** represents the hub of the wheel.

The tyre is what gives it the ability to go faster, and further and for longer. The tyre is in essence the **sales planning strategy** – without this, the unicycle would not be able to ride the distance safely.

The map / signposting – this acts as a guide showing you the routes you can take and can be compared to the **marketing / promotional strategy**. The map / signposting essentially shows you the different routes that you could follow to take you to various sales destinations.

I compare the routes to the many different forms of promotional activity that SMEs could do. When I say promotion, this can be sales, marketing, networking, advertising, social media, or the various types of marketing that are also methods in their own right – e.g. SEO, PR.

Developing a wheel that has a central hub, 8 spokes and a strong tyre, is what I believe small businesses need to develop and ride on if they want to succeed in what is an increasingly competitive sales market. Combine this with a good map and a plan of the initial routes to follow, and this is what should lead to early sales success.

It's all about doing the right things, at the right time, in the right way. This means focusing on developing the spokes and hub of the wheel first (foundational sales elements – encased in the website / showcase) which sit centrally to everything you do. Then adding the tyre (the sales planning strategy) and using your map / signposts to plan how you will get to your sales destinations and what routes to market you will use.

Figure 1: The UniC Sales Planning Wheel

The 4 routes I think should always be followed initially are low-cost and easily accessible to all SMEs. These are:

- Networking offline and online (requires an elevator pitch)
- LinkedIn, and one other social media channel – for general social media
- Social selling (LinkedIn)
- Local advertising and / or local promotional activity.

The Importance of the 'UniC Sales Planning Wheel' Approach

Getting sales, marketing and digital functions working cohesively is a vital component for sales success, and a good strategy is of paramount importance! Doing the right things, at the right time, in the right way, in the right order within the budget that's available can make an amazing difference to sales.

The Importance of the Hub / Website

Essentially, the central point of the wheel (your website – or the hub of the wheel) encapsulates all your sales foundations work and acts as a showcase, sales engine, salesperson, and content hub for your business.

This is because the 8 integral sales foundational elements (spokes) including target audience work, branding, messaging, story, keywords / SEO plan, service offering, USPs and trust signals feed directly into the hub and are encapsulated within it.

> Your website will display all your sales info for the world to see – things like your brand's backstory, tagline, info about the company, product / service offerings, values and pricing. The message it conveys will outline your USPs and the content will provide information about your products / services and all their features and benefits – alongside answers to frequently asked questions.

Your website should also display things like client testimonials, case studies and details of professional bodies you are part of. It is there as your sales and content hub to provide information, answer questions and build trust – just like a salesperson does with traditional sales activity.

It's also the display case for your brand, your brand story and information about you, your team and their values.

Undergoing the UniC sales planning process will help you position your business effectively in terms of its sales foundations and strategy, and these things then make up your UniC sales planning wheel which is represented in the real world by:

- your sales foundations and sales toolkit (spokes)
- your website (hub of wheel)
- your sales strategy (tyre of wheel)
- your marketing plan (route plan / map / signposting).

The Part Your Website (Hub) Plays

Having a good website (hub of the wheel) provides you with a central point around which all other activity can be directed. This enables you to put structure into your future sales and marketing and promotional activity.

Ultimately, a website should act as your sales brochure, your content hub and your online salesperson. All marketing / promotional roads lead to your website and it can be built to link with all your marketing / promotional activity in mind. It can also be developed / grown on an ongoing basis, and by doing this well it will make the website more and more powerful in terms of adding value to your sales and marketing activity (in several different ways).

I cannot emphasise enough how much value a good website can bring to a business.

I've often heard people talking up the value of just focusing on one social media channel without the need for a website. This is the opposite of what I believe.

My view is firstly never put all your eggs in one basket – especially one of the social media channels – as you don't own that basket! Your website should be yours (i.e. belong to your business). As a business owner this means you have control over it, and you can grow it from a content and SEO perspective on an ongoing basis without worry that what you develop could be taken away from you at any point.

> There is nothing more powerful in digital than a professionally well-built, sales-focused website, combined with a good sales and marketing strategy, because most promotional / marketing roads lead to your website.

What If You Can't Afford to Develop a Good Website at This Point?

A lot of small businesses cannot afford to develop a professional website from the outset. This does not matter to begin with as a professional website is essentially the display case for all the work that goes into the 8 foundational elements of the sales planning process (the spokes of the wheel).

As long as the sales foundations planning work is done effectively early on – then the display case (hub / website) can be constructed at any point once you have the budget for the work.

However, so that the sales planning wheel works from the outset, I think it's important to put a temporary website in place for low-cost early on. This may not last long or do a great job to showcase all the foundational elements like a professionally built website would, but it will at least allow the wheel to function.

The most important thing to do as early as possible is the initial foundational sales planning work for the 8 spokes of the wheel.

You can then create a very small website and a good LinkedIn page initially until you have made enough sales to have a professional website built.

By concentrating on the foundational elements of sales planning first and foremost, you will give yourself the opportunity to start making good sales through other means (e.g. networking, social selling, and a well-thought-out local sales strategy). This should lead to gaining the income required to construct an eye-catching, well-developed website as time progresses.

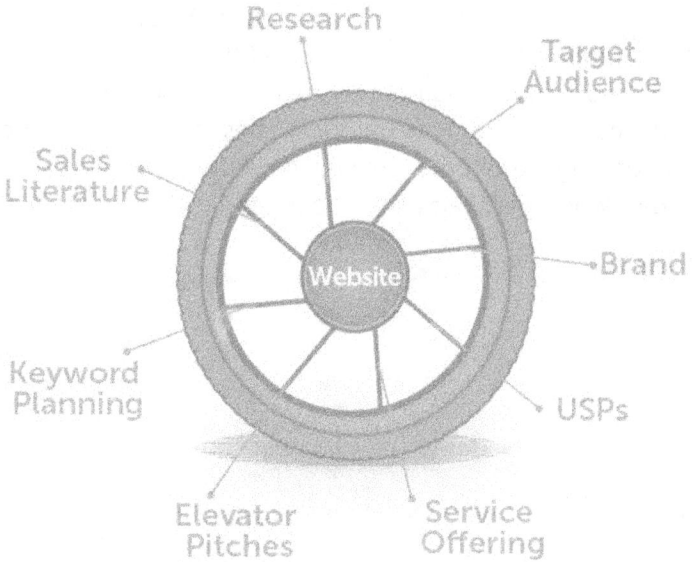

Research

Target
Audience

Sales
Literature

Website

Brand

Keyword
Planning

USPs

Elevator
Pitches

Service
Offering

PART 2:

THE 10-POINT UNIC SALES PLANNING PROCESS

CHAPTER 10:

The 10 Elements of Sales Planning: An Overview

In this section I will go through each of the points that make up the 10-point UniC sales planning process (which are listed below and on the next page).

1. What's your purpose and what are your key objectives?
2. Branding – naming and early branding elements (e.g. logo, design, tagline)
3. Building strong sales foundations – which breaks down into 8 areas:
   - Research and analysis
   - Target audience

- Brand identity and messaging
- Unique selling points (USPs)
- Product / service offering and packages
- Elevator pitches – coffee table, 60-second pitch, 3-minute pitch, 10-minute pitch
- Basic keyword planning
- Sales literature and visuals (graphics and images)

4. Sales toolkit
5. Networking insight and tips
6. Understanding the sales process
7. Overarching sales strategy / a hybrid approach
8. Social media / social selling
9. SEO planning
10. Website planning and content.

Why the 10-point UniC Sales Planning Process is So Beneficial

There are several reasons why this process is so beneficial for small business owners:

1. **Sales-focus** – it takes you through a step-by-step process to show you how to develop your brand / business effectively, with a focus on sales.
2. **Simplicity** – the process is orientated around keeping things simple, as that's what I believe works best for SMEs when it comes to sales. It's about going back to basics and aligning many elements of the traditional sales process with digital activity and the modern way of selling.
3. **Structure** – I think people tend to work better when they have structure. I know I function better in business and in day-to-day life when I have structure. This process is all about putting a structure into sales.

To summarise, the structure is focused around creating strong sales foundations (ideally encased in your website – your hub) and putting these at the heart of what you do sales-wise – so they sit centrally to all other promotional activity (as outlined in Figure 1 on page 107).

This gives you a central point for everything you do and a central point to build out from, strategically. You can feed into it from all your promotional channels, and you can feed out from it with all sorts of promotional material to be distributed via these channels.

4. **Strategy** – for the type of businesses this book is aimed at, having a strategic plan behind your sales activity is incredibly powerful and it's doing this that will deliver the best sales results.

   Ultimately, the 10-point UniC sales planning process is a methodology / process to help you create strong foundations, devise a good sales strategy that is budget-related, and take a measured and highly targeted approach to sales. This should help sales come in relatively quickly and enable you to take the cyclical approach to sales and marketing outlined on page 17.

5. **SEO (and other inbound marketing)** – if inbound marketing (and particularly SEO) is aligned to the sales hub (i.e. your sales foundations encased in your website) this will, over time, help improve sales.

   Whilst you may not be able to invest in ongoing SEO or inbound marketing activity immediately, the planning for the foundations of this should be done prior to the web development stage (not afterwards!) – so this is incorporated as part of the 10-point UniC sales planning process.

6. **Systematic** – I have devised what I believe to be a systematic method to follow which should help you create the strong foundations, structure and strategic planning you need to sell effectively on an ongoing basis. The system outlined in points 1–10 of the UniC sales planning process should be followed in order for best results.

7. **Sales toolkit** – by completing points 1–3 of the UniC sales planning process you should be able to produce a sales toolkit. This is a documented version of all the key things that I think you need to start selling effectively. It may require some specialist help to put a sales toolkit together properly. The details of what's contained in the toolkit are outlined on page 181.

There are three more terms that this planning system is based around.

8. **Symbiotic** – the whole process is built upon the idea that there should be a symbiotic approach to modern-day sales. What you do online should help your offline activity, and what you do offline should work with your online infrastructure – and the two should feed off each other for mutual gain and work in unison.

   It's a cyclical approach that starts with sales and this is why a hybrid activity is so important – particularly in the early days, but also throughout.

9. **Stress-free** – adopting the style and methods outlined in this process should enable you to start selling more naturally in a consultancy-style way and be more targeted, strategic and structured in your approach. These things combined should make the whole sales process far more stress-free.

10. Self-care – this sales planning process should give you the information and tools you require to start making sales activity much easier. However, business is always going to have tough times and sales will sometimes be hard, no matter how much you structure it, or how good at it you are. Knowing this is important, as you are likely to require patience and resilience to get through these times.

Taking care of your wellbeing is something I want to re-emphasise the importance of as I think the stronger we are in ourselves, the more resilience we have for the times when things do get more difficult.

Looking after our wellbeing and particularly our mental health is important for sales and business success, but crucially, it's important for us all as individuals.

> You can't sell if you're not well, so this 10-step process is most definitely supposed to be interspersed with regular breaks, walks in nature, time away from digital and from screens, and holidays. By following a systematic and structured approach to sales it should free some time up and allow you more free time to look after your wellbeing.

Not everyone is cut out to be a business owner and / or salesperson. If at any point you find the going gets too tough, then as I said before, getting out is not the same as giving up, and health must come first and foremost.

That said, getting there is far easier if you take care of yourself along the way. I think you have a much better chance of getting there and making a success of things sales-wise if you follow a structured approach that includes investing in yourself and your wellbeing.

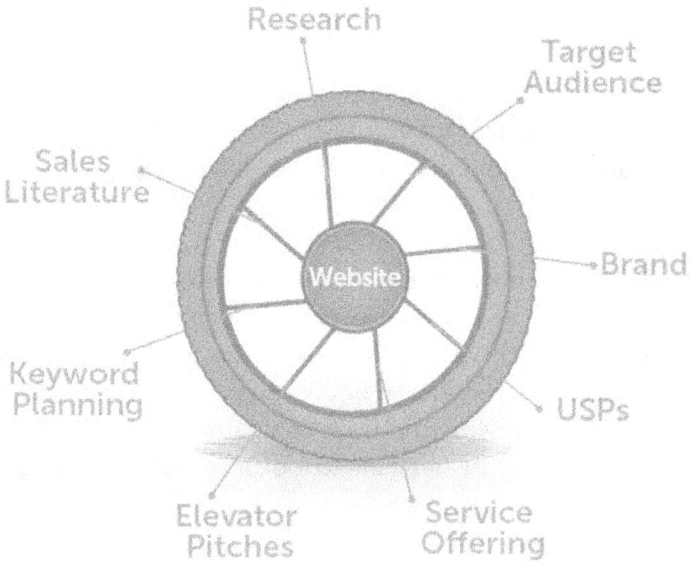

Research

Target
Audience

Sales
Literature

Website

Brand

Keyword
Planning

USPs

Elevator
Pitches

Service
Offering

CHAPTER 11:

Element 1: Your Purpose and Key Sales Objectives

As mentioned in the early chapters of the book, I think this is something that all small businesses should ask themselves before doing sales planning.

Essentially, you need to ask yourself what your purpose is in developing the business (i.e. where do you want your business growth to take you and what are your key objectives?).

To find this out, I think you need to ask yourself some questions, including this one.

What Type of Business Do You Want?

- A lifestyle business (one that just generates enough income to support you)
- A microbusiness without staff (a business that you grow slowly yourself by outsourcing or working alongside other small business owners)
- A microbusiness with 1 to 2 staff members that grows slowly
- A microbusiness that you grow to have a few employees – less than 10

- A reasonably sized SME with 10 or more employees
- A highly successful multi-million-pound business.

Whatever you decide your purpose and objectives for your business are, they need to be achievable.

You need to create the structure to enable you to reach the type of sales goals to do what you want. Your sales goals need to allow you to generate enough revenue to run your business effectively, maintain it, ensure it is profitable and grow it if that's what you want to do.

Ideally, it's best to ask these sorts of questions before you start your business, but it's something that can be done at any point. If you are an established business that wants to find ways to make more sales, then redefining your purpose can be done in line with rebranding and / or repositioning your brand, and / or embarking on a strategic sales process.

There is no right or wrong as to what is the perfect type of small business, but the bigger the business you want, the more sales you're likely to need to make. The more sales you need to make, the more funding and better infrastructure you'll need to get you there.

Salespeople cost money and so do many different forms of marketing that will be the types of marketing you would likely need to do to reach the high levels of sales required for bullet points 4, 5 and 6 above and on the previous page.

Also, there are likely to be all sorts of hurdles along the way when growing and scaling a business into a much bigger business. For example, it's not easy to find good salespeople, and if you do find them, they will need to be trained well which takes time, energy, focus and patience on both sides.

Running any business is hard, and employing and managing staff makes things a whole lot harder. So, I think there is a lot to be said for starting small and running a lifestyle or microbusiness initially if you don't have funding. Then, you can choose to grow if you want to a bit further down the line, rather than biting off more than you can chew.

Whatever size business you decide to develop, you need to have a very good idea of what your purpose is from the outset. This is because it's this knowledge that will help you develop the sales foundations and sales infrastructure of the business, so they are strong enough to support your business growth and achieve your goals.

If you build strong sales foundations as early as you possibly can, it should give you the sales springboard you need to generate sales on a regular basis. Then, the revenue gained from these early sales should enable you to go on and do different forms of marketing which should result in more sales.

Values

Some businesses will have a clear set of values from the outset. For example, they may be a locally based social enterprise-style business with a focus on raising awareness for a specific cause – e.g. mental health or helping mums get back to work. So, their values may be community, compassion, empowerment and communication (as examples).

All small businesses need brand values, not just social enterprises or those working in the field of good causes.

Values can be very different depending on what kind of business yours is. For example, customer care could be a number one value for some businesses. A different key value could be quality and producing quality products or services, or you might want your business to focus heavily on sustainability.

Working your business values out very early on in the sales planning process is important, as it helps you with branding, messaging and all sorts of other areas.

Taking Joy from the Journey

Knowing what your own values are as a person and a business owner is something I think is important to establish before you even start the sales planning process. This is because it can help you shape the size, style and sort of business you will run (or develop if you already have a business).

We work for a big chunk of our time, and for many of us, that can be eight hours a day or more, which is a substantial amount.

To me, this shouts out one message loud and clear. If you are going to start / develop / run and / or grow a business, you need to enjoy what you're doing, as you will spend a lot of time doing it! Ideally, you also want to develop it so the way you work fits neatly in with the other important aspects of your life.

This is very important, because if you enjoy what you do for a business, it makes the time that you put into it far more rewarding. It also allows you to take joy from the journey no matter how long it takes. I think emotionally and mentally this can be a really good way to progress in business instead of always looking to reach the summit of 'money mountain' that is notorious for being very hard to reach.

This same message translates very clearly to sales too. You are likely to make far more sales far more regularly if you enjoy the sales process. Ideally, you need to really believe in what you are selling and enjoy the sector you are working in, and like communicating with the types of people you plan to sell to.

What Drives You?

So, whether you are just starting out now, or want to improve your existing business so it makes more sales and / or makes you happier running it – it helps to think about the following:

- What things do you really enjoy doing?
- What inspires you?
- What ambitions do you have?
- What are you passionate about?

Ultimately, it's back to the point I made very early in the book – you need to have a clear idea of what success means to you.

If you are running a business, you need to know why you are doing it and dedicating so much time to it, which comes back to your values and what drives you.

If you can align your personal values and purpose with business purpose and sales planning, and get it to a point where there is some sort of crossover between the two, then I believe it will make business life more enjoyable. In turn, this is likely to help make it more successful and long-lasting.

The 10-point UniC sales planning process can be used by any business of any size at any stage of the journey. It's just harder to implement some of the elements when a business is more developed. But whatever the case, the first thing you need to do as a business owner is work out what your values and purpose are, and what those of the business are.

CHAPTER 12:

Element 2: Branding and Brand Development

Branding

Branding and brand development are two different things.

In the SME market, I think it's safe to say that branding is generally focused on the visual elements of your 'brand' – the impression it creates, the core message it delivers and how memorable it is.

Branding incorporates things like the logo, design, brand name and tagline. I think the branding / rebranding process (for existing businesses) should occur alongside sales planning and the two should ideally happen simultaneously.

One problem that seems to happen a lot in the SME sector, is many small business owners fall at the very first hurdle and don't do these important first steps of branding / sales planning properly.

They don't think about the importance of a brand name, domain name, logo or other elements of branding. This is such an unnecessary mistake to make as these things can be done relatively cheaply.

The irony is that aside from sales planning and a good website, your brand name and branding are probably two of the most important investments you can make in relation to sales.

Most branding specialists will be quick to tell you that branding is far more complex than creating a name and logo though, and they are right.

This is because to produce strong branding, you must first have in-depth knowledge of what makes up 'the brand'. This means lots of work needs to go into understanding the business, its mission, its values and its target audience way before any branding concepts can be created.

The considerations mentioned make up part of the sales planning process too and I think this is why branding should be done in line with sales planning, or after some of the early sales planning work has taken place.

If you are an established business and you overlooked branding when you started out, it doesn't matter. Rebranding and sales planning can always be done after you have been running for a few years — it's just more complex.

Brand Development

I believe brand development takes the whole process of branding many steps further than a logo and tagline. My definition of brand development is that 'it's the ongoing work that is done to develop a brand effectively from conception and throughout the life of the brand'.

As part of brand development, much of the information gleaned from the initial sales planning and branding processes will be used.

In my view, successful brand development means developing every aspect of your brand / business effectively. The objective being to make it strong from the start from a sales perspective and position it well, so it helps raise brand awareness and drive enquiries through different forms of promotional activity (sales, marketing, advertising, networking, social media etc.).

Please note, if you are an existing business and don't like your branding, it may not be advisable to try and change your brand name – as there are a lot of reasons that this may not be a good idea, as mentioned previously.

But don't worry, as you can always reposition a brand to make more impact sales-wise without having to change the name / domain name.

Every interaction the user has with the brand, both online and offline, should be considered going forward from a brand development perspective. So, if you create any marketing material, advertising material, promotional material, such as exhibition stands etc., the brand and branding need to be considered.

It should also be considered during any direct sales activity, e.g. elevator pitches, networking, social selling, meetings, sales presentations / pitches.

Continuity of branding and brand values are important as you grow your business, and it's useful to create brand guidelines from the outset.

To summarise, I'd say brand development is how you develop your brand online and offline – pretty much all the things you do to build and grow it.

Brand Development and Sales

With so many channels, platforms and marketing methods to consider, effective brand development is an ongoing process. For small businesses in the SME sector, these days the growth of the business and the brand from a sales and marketing perspective is so closely interlinked it's often almost the same thing.

There are multiple reasons why good brand development is important in relation to sales. Five key reasons are:

- To make a visual impact
- To maintain continuity and memorability. Like I said before, I see the brand / brand development as a fine chain running through everything you do and it's the thing that holds your offline and online promotional activity together
- To build trust
- To evoke feeling
- To encourage interaction.

In the small business marketplace, it is the generation of new business (i.e. sales) that is generally the primary purpose of brand development – if you develop your brand well it should be a powerful tool to help you deliver sales.

Good branding and brand development does of course help raise brand awareness too, but unless you have very deep pockets to invest large sums in digital activity and promotional activity like TV, this is unlikely to be the primary benefit for SMEs. When it comes to the small business market, the primary benefit is generally to help make sales.

What is Brand Planning?

So where does brand planning fit in? I define brand planning as 'the creation of the strategy for the successful development of a brand'. So, whereas brand development is the branding, sales, marketing and digital activity you undertake to develop your brand, it is brand planning that is the process you need to go through to plan this.

Brand planning is the well-thought-out planning of several areas of development and promotional activity that will help you raise awareness of your brand and produce 'sales' cost effectively. I consider brand planning to be heavily sales-focused because the purpose of brand planning for most SMEs is to help drive sales and deliver a good ROI (return on investment).

Brand planning is what I class as the umbrella term to describe the things a business needs to plan (devise strategies for) to develop their brand effectively and generate sales. This includes sales planning, marketing planning, digital planning, SEO / inbound planning and advertising strategy (media planning).

Brand planning is so important for sales, it's why I named my company Brand Planning Ltd. My definition of this term refers to all the sales-focused strategic and development planning for the key areas I have outlined in the table on the next page.

Brand planning breaks down into 5–6 sub-sectors and, because sales is so integral to the brand development strategy, it is the sales planning sub-sector which is the most dominant (see Figure 2 on the next page).

How 'Brand Planning' Breaks Down

Sales Planning	Digital Planning	SEO Planning	Marketing Planning	Media Planning
Sales objectives	Apps	Keywords	Email / newsletters	Print ads
Branding	eBooks	Content	Content marketing	Digital ads
Sales foundations		Digital PR	Social media	Social ads
Sales toolkit and sales materials		Tech	PR	Offline – events etc
Networking			Video	TV and radio
Hybrid sales strategy			Events	Outdoor
Website and web content planning			Personal branding	Sponsorship
Social selling – includes social media pages			Podcasting	PPC
ABM – Account-based marketing				
Basic SEO foundational work				

Figure 2: How 'Brand Planning' Breaks Down

Note: I have put ABM under sales planning, and this is because whilst it is referred to as a marketing activity, I believe it is a sales-related activity.

Also, I have included website planning and social media pages under sales planning, as whilst I class these as 'digital materials' as far as planning goes, they are so integral to the sales process and so intertwined with other elements of the sales foundational work that it's most appropriate for them to sit under the sales planning sub-sector. Figure 2 includes most key areas of brand planning that I consider important for small businesses, but there may be more that could be added.

The Brand Planning Approach

Sales planning and the 10-point UniC sales planning process (which are the main focus of this book) are elements of the wider brand planning approach.

Branding elements fall under the sales planning sub-sector because I believe that branding and brand development must be considered every step of the way throughout the sales planning process. Then also in every aspect of the ongoing sales process.

The brand, and brand name / domain, are 2 key elements of the sales foundations and are attached to the website (which encases the sales foundations), and they sit centrally within the sales planning wheel as shown in Figure 1 on page 107.

Making sure you have strong branding from the outset is one of the first considerations in the 10-point UniC sales planning process as the strength of your brand counts for so much when it comes to raising brand awareness and making sales.

As I explained before, I see the branding as a fine chain running through everything a small business / brand does from a sales / marketing and promotional perspective, and it's what holds everything together as it spreads outwards from the central hub (the website, which is the home of the brand).

It then spreads through every aspect of the wider ongoing marketing and promotional strategies that make up the other sub-sectors of brand planning.

A focus on brand planning and brand development in everything you do allows you to take a cohesive and consistent approach to sales, marketing, promotion and digital development. By following the 10-point UniC sales planning process, the sales planning sub-sector is the key area of focus and at the heart of this sits the sales planning wheel.

Some of the earliest things that are likely to be considered on the brand development side of things will be business cards, social media pages, a small website and some sales materials, as these are all necessary for sales to be made.

Your Brand Name

From a branding and brand development perspective, the name of your business / brand is very important, and in the digital world this means ensuring you get a good domain name.

I firmly believe that your brand / domain name and your website (which your domain name will be attached to) are the most powerful sales and marketing tools you will ever have. So, that's why it's so important to think so seriously about this area.

What Do You Do If You Already Have a Brand but Don't Think it's Working Well?

My answer to this is you could potentially change a brand name or business name, but this would take research, thought, planning and looking into any legalities properly.

Often the work / hassle to do this will simply be too much. Or the SEO risk could be too great. If either of these things are the case, then it may be far better to maintain an existing brand name but position it much more effectively.

Doing this is likely to mean having a full redesign including new logo, new colours, new tagline and core messaging. So, it is still the same brand but produces a far more powerful impact from both a branding and sales perspective.

It does not matter where you are in your business journey, it is usually possible for specialists to find a great way to brand, rebrand and / or reposition your brand, so it has strong sales-focused foundations and a powerful and effective impact.

Where Will Your Brand Name / Domain Name Appear?

The main reason your brand name is so important is because it will appear on almost every form of sales and marketing activity that you do.

Overleaf are some examples of the things your domain name is likely to regularly appear on if you promote your business effectively:

- Your business cards
- Your website
- Your email address
- The footer of your emails
- Sales literature and PDFs
- Marketing material such as flyers
- Your social media pages
- Social media posts
- Organic search results (SEO results)
- PPC results
- The business page of your LinkedIn profile
- Your LinkedIn personal profile
- Your elevator pitches
- Exhibition stands
- Promotional materials – T-shirts, pens, pads etc
- Directory listings (or listings on other web properties)
- Your invoices and similar material
- Videos
- Podcasts
- Radio / TV appearances
- Press releases
- Editorial articles
- Guest posts
- Testimonials that you write about people and people write about you
- Advertising
- PR activity
- Books
- eBooks
- Downloadable materials
- Courses.

The list is endless.

Essentially, your brand (or business name) should appear on almost everything you create and do, particularly any sales, marketing and promotional materials.

When you look at the list on the previous page, it quickly becomes apparent how vitally important it is for sales to have a strong and memorable brand name and a good website.

How Do You Rebrand / Reposition Your Name Effectively?

If it's difficult to change your brand name, then how you reposition your business from a branding perspective when you undergo sales planning is more important than ever.

Rebranding can help you improve your logo, tagline, values, messaging, images and visual impact and enable you to reposition your brand effectively.

For example, you could somehow incorporate a tagline that always sits alongside the name in the branding that brings rationale to the name you're using but makes people focus more heavily on the tagline.

It's amazing what branding specialists can do to revitalise, strengthen and turnaround an existing name from something that you dislike and that brings you no value to something you fall in love with and that brings you a renewed sense of confidence in your business and the desire to promote your brand as heavily as you can.

So, all is certainly not lost if you need to keep your existing brand name – it can most likely be rebranded effectively. The one thing I'd say you need to be prepared to do if this is your situation though is pay a decent amount to use a good branding specialist or agency.

To do this type of rebranding and repositioning work effectively usually takes a great deal of experience and expertise. But I'd say it's something that is well worth investing in because good branding adds so much value to the sales process.

Why a Strong Brand Name Can Help with Offline Sales

- **Networking and meeting people at events** – an easy-to-remember brand name (or good brand / tagline) helps people remember you even if they only meet you briefly – it can also be a great conversation starter as when people read your business card they may ask about the name or tagline if it is good.

- **For elevator pitches** – ending an elevator pitch by including your brand name and web address can work well in terms of enticing people to visit your website.

- **For radio appearances, podcasts, video etc.** – if your brand name is easy to say and memorable then it is an amazing promotional tool to use on any of these things.

- **Print advertising** – using print for promotional and advertising activity can be a low cost and effective form of promotion for small businesses, especially when done locally. A good brand name and / or a memorable brand can help greatly with this type of promotion.

Benefits of Strong Brand Positioning in Relation to Sales

- **Create memorability** – a good brand name like the name of my business, 'Brand Planning Ltd', can help in terms of memorability. When you say it to people, whether this be at networking, social events, or a different form of advertising, they are likely to remember it and be able to find it easily.

- **Clarity** – a good, strong brand name (i.e. one that is succinct and memorable) means that people are likely to hear what you say more easily and hear the name clearly when it is read out. This can help at networking events, and if you or your team appear on radio, TV, podcasts, video etc.

- **Sales confidence** – if you like your brand and feel confident that it quickly relays the message of what your business does, then this in turn can help give you more confidence when you are doing sales pitches etc.

  When you are proud of something this can be reflected in your tone of voice and your mannerisms, and the whole way you present something. So, having a strong brand is an important consideration when it comes to sales confidence.

- **Leverage** – if you feel your brand sounds stronger and makes a better first impression than the competition, this can also help give you sales leverage. Bigger is not always the best, and a strong brand can give even the smallest business sales leverage, in terms of how the business can be positioned and presented.

Your Logo

An important element of creating a strong brand identity is having a great logo and design features so that visually you deliver a strong image. First impressions count for so much in so many aspects of sales and marketing. The visual impact of your brand is therefore very important.

Your logo is likely to be the first thing your potential client sees, so having a distinctive and well-designed logo is vital. It will appear on your website and on a lot of your sales and marketing material.

Also, if you do any press activity or promotional activity for directories, podcasts, printed magazines etc. you will often be asked to send a copy of your logo for them to promote you on their media properties and throughout social media.

The better the logo, the greater the impact. Logos are something that can potentially be changed relatively easily – so if you have had yours for a while and want a new one then it could be time for a logo redesign.

Your Tagline

A tagline is something that can be used to get the message of your brand across in one sentence. Creating good taglines is quite an art. I think they need to be clever, but simple and short, and say a lot.

Personally, I think taglines are usually more important for bigger businesses that spend a lot on advertising – and you will see that taglines really come into play on TV adverts and radio adverts with big companies – but I think it's good for businesses of any size to have a good tagline from the start, as you never know at what point it's going to come in useful.

Taglines are great to use at networking events during an elevator pitch and in adverts, flyers, press advertising etc. As I mentioned earlier, they can also help bring cohesion between an existing brand name and the core messaging of the business.

Taglines become especially useful if you have an existing brand name that cannot be changed but you want to reposition your brand more effectively.

It may seem like one or two sentences is a small thing. However, creating a great tagline early in the sales planning process that defines your brand succinctly and with a bit of clever word play is another fantastic tool for your sales toolkit.

Why Not Just Do Personal Branding?

I think there is too much talk on social media channels about personal branding and that too many small business owners focus on personal branding and overlook business branding.

For those that don't know, personal branding is essentially raising awareness of an individual (e.g. the business owner / founder) and bringing attention to what they believe in and have to say etc.

I genuinely think personal branding can be fantastic at times, but my views on this in relation to small businesses making sales are as follows:

- Unless you really do have the potential to become a thought leader or influencer in your field, I think personal branding could be a hard thing to do effectively.

- I also think it's likely to take a long time to build a personal brand because it takes a lot of work and appearances on podcasts, radio etc. and copious amounts of social media activity.
- It probably helps if you have a book or online course etc. (but doing any of these things takes time and money – writing books takes a great deal of time...believe me!).
- I would say the cross-channel approach (i.e. using several methods of promotion offline and online) is harder with personal branding.
- Finally, if you're aiming for influencer status by building a personal brand that has a high volume of social media followers, this means building that high volume following – which in some ways goes against the strategy of a quality over quantity sales approach that I talk about with the UniC 10-point sales planning process.

My view is that for most small business owners, personal branding should be done after or alongside the business brand development – I don't think it should take the place of the business brand.

I have rather strong views about this because I am an SEO / inbound marketing specialist as well as a sales professional. I think having a good business website (and strategically planning early on for the future of inbound marketing) should be one of the most important aspects of a sales-focused sales / marketing plan for many SMEs.

So, whilst I'd encourage personal brand development for those businesses that it is right for (my own being one of them), I don't ever think it should be done instead of business branding. I think business branding should come first and foremost, and that personal branding should be something the business owner does after / alongside this.

There is one overriding reason for this, and that is because your website sits centrally to every aspect of promotional activity that you do, and if you are running a business, I believe it is the business website that should sit centrally for a multitude of reasons.

For example, if I were to appear on a podcast, while this might happen to build up my personal profile and may generate followers on social media (which would help my personal brand), I would still want to direct people to my business website as I would be appearing as the founder of my business.

It would be my business website I would mention during discussions and if I was asked to give out a web address.

Also, if the host was doing pre- or post-event promotion, I would provide them with info about me (in relation to the session) as the founder of my business – but the website details would be those of the business.

This way, it is essentially a double benefit. The business website remains as the central point, but by making appearances on podcasts or radio etc. I would be naturally promoting my 'personal brand' too.

There are other reasons for not putting too much emphasis on personal branding:

- You don't own social media channels, so if you are predominantly building a personal brand on a particular social media platform, I would say that is a very risky thing to do. What happens if something happens to the social media channel, or they decide for some unknown reason to block your account?

- If you are thinking about merging or selling your business anytime in the future, then the brand will be important, and an acquirer is unlikely to want to buy a personal brand – as by its sheer nature, it is personal to you!

CHAPTER 13:

Element 3: Sales Foundations (8 Key Areas)

Strong sales foundations are pivotal – as these are the things that need to be in place to allow you the best chance of generating sales enquiries.

Sales foundations are essentially the strong base that is required to maximise returns from the time and energy put into any sales, marketing, advertising and promotional activity that you do.

In line with the 10-point UniC sales planning process, once you have a good website (hub) it should encase all the planning of your sales foundations, provide a showcase for these, and sit centrally to everything else you do.

The sales foundations and website create a strong base for everything you do sales- and marketing-wise and give you a springboard from which to sell effectively. It's also what maximises returns from marketing activity – i.e. people that see the marketing activity get directed to the foundational elements (e.g. website) and see good sales messaging and, as a result, the marketing budget is more effective and produces a better ROI.

Most promotional / marketing routes feed into the website and it also gives you a central point to feed out from (promotionally) – i.e. snippets of blogs can be fed out to other marketing channels, but they reside on the website. Snippets of videos could be fed out to other channels as a teaser, with a link to the whole video which sits on the website etc.

In my mind, a good website is like building a property – if you create strong foundations for a property from the outset, you can build higher and higher and higher – it's the same with a website, except a website tends to expand outwards as opposed to upwards. So, a better analogy is perhaps a tree – with the foundations being the roots, the homepage the trunk, the top-level pages the main branches from which hundreds and thousands of smaller branches can grow.

Strong sales foundations give you the base from which to sell more and more over time, and this gives you leverage from which to develop your brand and grow it in a similar way to which a property built on strong foundations grows.

Key Elements of Sales Foundations

On the next page is a list of the 8 key elements of the sales foundations section of the 10-point UniC sales planning process.

These are the key things that need to be planned to create strong foundations. These 8 elements are what become encased in a website when things are developed well in line with the 10-point UniC sales planning process.

Over the following pages I will talk you through each of these foundational elements in detail.

- Research and analysis
- Target audience
- Branding – identity and messaging
- Unique selling points (USPs)
- Product / service offering and packages
- Elevator pitches – coffee table, 60-second pitch, 3-minute pitch, 10-minute pitch
- Basic keyword planning
- Sales literature and visuals (graphics and images).

Research and Analysis

Competitor Analysis

Doing some competitor analysis will give you an overview of the competitors in your market, which will help you if you are trying to decide what brand name to call your business and how to position your brand effectively.

Just because other companies are bigger or have been trading longer, it does not necessarily mean that their brand name, logo, design, branding positioning or digital marketing infrastructure is good. Sometimes companies overlook these important factors.

If you know who the competition is, it will help you analyse and draw comparisons with existing brands, and this information should give you a steer on how to develop your brand to compete.

Know Your Competition and What Differentiates You from Them

Knowing who your competition is, how they operate, how they promote themselves, what image they are portraying, what their services and price points are, and what their USPs are can help you position all these things for your business more effectively.

Understanding as much as you can about 4–5 competitors allows you to see their strengths and weaknesses. In turn, this helps you to ascertain how to position your business most effectively against your direct competition.

Things to look at when doing competitor analysis are:

- How long have they been running?
- Do they have a website?
- Does the website give a good first impression?
- Is the website easy to navigate?
- Is the website informative?
- What services do they offer?
- Do they have packages?
- What is their pricing like?
- What is their target market?
- Do they have a strong brand name?
- Do they have a good LinkedIn presence?
- How many people are in their team?
- How local are they to you?
- What kind of keywords are they appearing for in searches?
- Do they specialise in a niche?
- Do they have good recommendations / testimonials?
- Have they won awards?
- Do they operate in a wider area than you?

Once you have done this initial competitor analysis work you can then spend some time giving thought to the following:

- What services do you offer that they don't?
- What things do you do that they don't?
- How do your prices compare?

- If your prices are cheaper then great, that's a good selling point. However, if they're more expensive, you need to think about why and decide how to position this.

SWOT Analysis

A SWOT analysis is another thing that you can do to help in the sales planning process. This means looking at your business with sales in mind and thinking about its **S**trengths, **W**eaknesses, **O**pportunities and **T**hreats from a sales perspective. This can include things like strength of your experience as a business owner.

The purpose of doing a sales-focused SWOT analysis at this stage is to give you a clearer idea of all the positive things you have going for you and your business, and to identify areas that need work. It also gives you a chance to see the opportunities that are available to you and the threats that might be a potential problem.

Doing a SWOT analysis focused on sales is a great way to get you thinking about the standing of your business from a sales perspective and how it can be improved.

With many small businesses, many of the points that often appear in the weaknesses section of the SWOT analysis will be the same. Often what is missing (and thus a weakness) is many of the key things that need to be done to build strong sales foundations from both an offline and online digital perspective.

It's also worth looking at external threats – i.e. things that could occur as a threat that are beyond your control as a business owner – such as economic downturn.

Target Audience

One of the biggest mistakes that I think small business owners make these days is that they don't target effectively.

Instead, they approach things without having thought about who their target audience is, or what their niche is, and this results in low enquiries and a poor ROI.

Basically, time and money gets wasted time and time again because people hope that some of the social media and marketing activity they do will stick.

They are not actually sourcing the right type of audience to put their message in front of. Not in the same way that traditional salespeople did when they used to trawl through magazines, newspapers and lists to find their leads.

Sales planning not only helps you understand how to sell effectively, but it also helps you decide what approach you should take for marketing the products and / or services you want to sell. There are so many different marketing options and approaches that it is important to have a strategy to go in the right direction (in line with budget availability). Good sales planning helps you to do this.

There are lots of things that need to be taken into consideration when it comes to both offline and online sales. Many of these things only apply to digital, but there are many elements of traditional sales that cross over into the online market.

These areas include identifying your USPs (unique selling points), deciding on your target market and the key types of decision-makers that you want to contact / connect with.

In marketing you tend to look at customer personas, but in sales I would say it's more important to give more thought to who your typical decision-maker is likely to be that you want to sell to.

For example, is it business owners, marketing managers or HR managers?

Your Target Market

It's very important that you understand who your target audience is, know where to find them, and have a strategy to either get in front of them, or get them to come to you so you can deliver your sales messages to them.

Here are some useful points to consider:

- For SMEs, sales success is best achieved by having a good strategy and doing the right sales and marketing activity at the right time to the right people.
- I believe defining the right audience and targeting them effectively is a necessity for sales success for most SMEs. This is one area where there is a lot of crossover between sales and marketing.
- Personally, I think when sales and marketing are working in unison, sales should be about defining the right audience and creating core sales messaging for this audience. It's about understanding who they are, what drives them, and what their needs and pain points are. It's also about direct 121 interaction to relay this messaging.
- I tend to think the messaging that relates to sales is any message that is either static, or on something that you send out or hand out on individual request. So, the messaging on your website, for example, and your landing pages and

social media pages is what I would class as sales-related as it is static.

- Sales materials such as PDFs and other materials that get requested or given out to individuals are also what I would class as sales-related. As are tailored direct messages sent to individuals after you have made an initial introduction – these could be via social selling or email.

- Marketing on the other hand should be about devising the strategy to get in front of the target audience (or to get them to come to you - e.g. via SEO) and finding creative ways to deliver the core sales messaging.

- Many marketers will be adamant that targeting is part of marketing which it is, but it is a key element of sales too. With most small businesses I firmly believe it should start with defining the target audience from a sales perspective first, as without doing so you cannot create solid and strong sales foundations.

- Marketing messages tend to get sent out / delivered en masse. So, social media posts, email newsletters, social media newsletters and direct mail all go out en masse so I will count these types of things as marketing material / messages. It's important to note however, that this type of marketing activity will often have sales messages within it – this is one of the things that I think creates a lot of confusion between sales and marketing.

- Essentially, to undertake sales and / or marketing effectively, you need to have a good understanding of your target audience and have a plan as to how you will reach them.

- Sales and marketing are independent disciplines but have a common goal and by working in conjunction with one another, I believe the results will always be better.

Why Choose a Niche?

When I talk about targeting and niche marketing, I am referring to two different things, but there is a lot of crossover.

- **Targeting** – deciding upon the type of audience you want to get your message in front of via sales and marketing activity – i.e. what sectors / type of businesses you want to appeal to and who the type of typical buyers within these businesses are.

- **Niching or specialising** – deciding what your key areas of focus for your business will be from a sales and marketing perspective – i.e. what categories / sectors you will specialise in. For example, I'm a sales, marketing and digital specialist but my business focuses more heavily on one niche, which is sales.

I believe these two things are incredibly important elements of a successful sales strategy for B2B service and high-value product businesses.

Targeting has always been a key component of traditional sales and marketing. For example, businesses used to promote themselves in trade magazines that were distributed to a very focused specific audience, or via direct mail which was location-specific, and which utilised demographic data to target to a granular level.

In fact, this type of offline marketing / advertising (and similar offline methods) can still be very beneficial, but these things are not that often considered as potential options by SMEs because digital marketing (particularly social media) steals the limelight.

As a generalisation, social media activity is a classic example of how businesses don't target effectively on digital channels. It seems that many SMEs don't consider their target audience when using social media. I don't think this is a good way to go as using social media without thinking about targeting is like throwing paint against a wall and just seeing what sticks.

Poorly optimised websites, blogs, newsletters and landing pages are all other examples of digital activity that often give no thought to targeting, or to conversion rate optimisation for that matter.

Badly planned PPC and paid ads often don't work that well either because targeting has not been thought about in enough detail and landing pages are poor due to this.

The irony of all of this is that digital activity, when done well, can be highly targeted. In addition, it's the most measurable form of marketing there is.

Effective Targeting

I think effective targeting is pivotal to sales (and marketing) success if you are a business owner that has a relatively low budget for marketing.

Effective targeting starts with good planning and, for various reasons, I think it needs to be done at the sales planning stage.

- Understanding your target audience is required to build strong sales foundations.
- Understanding your niche is required to build strong sales foundations.
- Keywords for use in web content and SEO can only be planned once you have a good understanding of your niche and target market.

- Social media pages are important for social selling, but they need to be written with the target audience in mind to be most effective.
- Website pages are very important for targeted marketing to be effective.
- Landing pages are important for PPC activity (paid search) and need to be planned around the target market too.

The Benefits of Targeting and Niching for SMEs

The simple answer is that it helps you appeal to the right audience and make more sales! Effective targeting and niching have a wealth of benefits. Below are just a few.

- You have much more chance of generating warm leads (i.e. enquiries from people who may have a genuine interest) if you target effectively. Warm leads are the easiest enquiries to turn into sales as often the person making the enquiry is in buying mode.

- Niching effectively enables you to focus more heavily on one or two specialist areas, which has all sorts of advantages when it comes to targeting, social selling and inbound marketing / SEO too. It also helps you be more strategic with your sales plan for networking activity etc.

- If you niche / specialise it helps your business to start being recognised as a specialist in your field. This helps build trust, gain recommendations etc. and enables you to be strategic and focused with both your sales strategy and your content creation.

  This is very beneficial for sales as if people don't buy immediately, they may well start remembering you. They might bookmark your posts or website, and they might sign up to your newsletter because your niche area is of real interest to them.

- Focusing on a niche and becoming known for it can start to open doors for you. You may be able to appear on podcasts and talk about your areas of specialism, which in turn helps raise more awareness. This is because other people may share information of the podcast through their networks – this in turn will help you gain more enquiries that could turn into sales. This is particularly true if your website is full of informative info relating to you, your business and your niche area of focus.

- By niching (specialising in a specific area) it opens up possibilities for you to become a thought leader in your area of specialism. In turn, this will open more doors and get your information shared more readily, which again can help with sales.

- Writing lots of content around a specific area (niche) also makes it easier to repurpose content. This helps your marketing, but it also helps you save time, and this is a precious commodity for small business owners who are trying to make sales.

- Specialising in a particular area has a major impact on content planning and writing too. In turn, this has a positive impact on future SEO that you may do, even if it's only blog writing to begin with. I think focusing on a niche and a specific target market makes SEO easier and more likely to be successful for various reasons. Good SEO results impact sales positively as they tend to lead to warm enquiries, which as I said before are the best type of enquiries to turn into sales.

- Specialising in a niche area helps with PR and digital PR too, which are two things that can potentially be done for low cost. These areas can help raise more awareness with the right target audience, which can lead to more warm enquiries. When done well, digital PR also has a positive impact on search engine optimisation.

- Having a specialism / niche helps with all sorts of elements of the traditional side of selling too – i.e. finding the right type of prospects, networking activity. It also helps greatly with your social selling activity (which is essentially networking / sales activity online on social platforms) and account-based marketing, which I see as essentially being sales.

Finding Your Niche

Giving real thought to how you might focus on a particular niche and who your target audience should be are key elements of the early sales planning process.

I believe small business owners should go for quality over quantity in every aspect of sales and marketing work they do.

I think on social media it's important to look for quality connections and prospects, as opposed to quantity. Finding the right type of connections to connect with and / or follow as opposed to a high volume of random connections has a wealth of benefits.

I think that sales for B2B service businesses and / or high-value product businesses is about building strong foundations, having a well-planned sales and marketing strategy and then getting in front of as many of the right prospects as possible.

The important words in the previous sentence to me are not 'as many' but instead are the words 'the right'.

Yes, I believe making sales is down to volume – the more people that get to know about your services / product range the better, but it must be the right type of people.

I'd much rather the services my business, Brand Planning Ltd, offers were seen by 100 of the right type of prospects than 1000 people that did not fit my target client criteria as a business owner.

How Do You Establish Your Target Audience?

So, how do you know how to define your target audience and who the right prospects are?

This is where good sales planning comes in.

I think it's incredibly hard to work out who your ideal prospects are until you have a real understanding of your business and product / service offering.

Below and on the next page are just some of the questions I work with clients on to help them gain a clearer idea of their business and service offering with a view to working out who their target prospects should be.

How Many of These Questions Can You Answer?

- What are you selling?
- Who do you want to buy your service / products?
- What are your niche areas of focus?
- What are the features of your product / service?
- What are the general benefits of your product / service?

- Who is your competition and how do you compare to the competition?
- What are your unique selling points as a business and for your services?
- What is your price point?
- How are you planning to sell your service or product?
- What's your monthly sales and marketing budget?
- What are the strengths / weaknesses of your offering?
- What specialist sector knowledge do you have?
- What packages do you sell?

Sales is not simple – initially there is a lot to it, and ensuring the foundational elements are planned and developed well helps immensely. Sales becomes easier the stronger your foundations and sales planning are.

I also think that your sales foundations and sales planning become stronger when you have a clear idea of your target audience and your niche.

Hopefully, the above questions will help you to start to think more strategically about making sales and defining your target audience and niche area of focus.

Why Sales Before Marketing is So Important

I think sales is more important than marketing for several reasons – three of the key ones are below and on the next page:

- Sales is what brings in revenue, and revenue is what keeps a business afloat and helps it grow.
- Money made from sales can be ploughed into other areas of marketing to help increase sales on an ongoing basis, but

this only works well if strong sales foundations and a good sales strategy are in place.
- Marketing is unlikely to produce many sales without sales foundations work and / or sales interaction (by a salesperson / business owner).

If you are a small business with limited funds, the thing to remember is that your business can essentially grow through good sales activity alone. It does not require marketing to make sales.

As far as I'm concerned, sales should be the primary consideration for small business owners, but if budget allows, I firmly believe sales and marketing should always work together, with continual cohesion through the sales, marketing and digital mix.

Branding – Identity and Messaging

To build any brand successfully you need to create a brand identity. This is essentially how you want to position your brand to other people and how you want them to perceive it.

The brand values you decide on for your business should be incorporated into your brand identity. For example, if two of your key values are luxury and quality then these will become part of your brand identity.

An important part of creating a 'brand identity' is tone of voice – i.e. the words you use to describe your brand and deliver your brand message(s) to your target audience.

What words you choose to use is therefore a very important consideration and you want to avoid getting it wrong, as you wouldn't want the wrong words to be associated with your brand.

For example, if your brand is a luxury brand and you want to attract an affluent audience, you are unlikely to want to ever use words like 'cheap' or 'low cost' to describe your product / service.

However, something could potentially be a luxury product / service but still be good value, so you will probably need to decide whether you will use these terms in your content.

Deciding on a list of adjectives that will be used and those that won't ever be used, prior to embarking on any form of sales messaging, can be helpful.

The strength of your brand and how it is presented are key components of making a great first impression.

> Your brand can speak volumes about your business before you even get the chance to make a first impression sales-wise yourself, so ensuring your brand helps sell your business with the first impression it makes online is extremely important.

Brand Story

There is a lot of talk about storytelling and how it's extremely important. I do think storytelling adds a lot of value when building a brand, but I think there are many things involved in developing a good brand, and storytelling is just one element.

Knowing what your business story is and having good background information ready about the story of your business / brand can help you in many ways and can positively impact sales.

- It can help you create pages on your website that will enable readers to get to know the brand better. This helps build a connection and trust and, in turn, this can help sales.
- On social media channels, sometimes, posts that are very authentic and tell the story of the growth of your brand and the personal struggles associated with this have far greater impact than posts that are less authentic and more business-like. This is not always the case – it does depend, but good storytelling can work well on social media.
- It can help you create sales and marketing material using elements of your story to draw people in and evoke emotion.
- Having a strong backstory can also help you when pitching and selling your brand directly, as it helps people relate to you, what you've been through, and how passionate you are about your brand and business growth.
- It can help with PR activity, particularly locally or in small magazines etc.
- With microbusinesses (businesses with a small number of employees), a big part of the backstory could incorporate the founders' biographies and experiences they have had to go through to get the business to where it is. This can help your target audience relate to you, and it can evoke a sense of trust.

Storytelling can take place across all sorts of channels and on various forms of sales marketing material, and can play a big part in the early sales process and can be done for low cost.

Here are some examples of where brand storytelling can be used:

- Website
- Networking events – particularly in longer elevator pitches (3 minutes)
- Video – for use on your website, other websites etc
- Social media posts
- Sales pitches and meetings

- Sales literature
- Books (for example, you've heard some of my story in this book)
- Podcasts.

I think if you are going to invest time in creating posts and promotional activity (e.g. PR) where you relay elements of your 'story', it's far better to do this once you have a strong brand, a good LinkedIn profile and a good website in place (all of which require elements of the 10-point UniC sales planning process to be done first).

Storytelling does cross over with personal branding as well. However, if you position things so you can incorporate elements of your personal story within your business promotional activity, this has more of a double-sided gain. It helps promote the business as people will warm to the founder's story – but it also helps start to position the founder(s) from a personal branding perspective too. This is good for future thought-leadership opportunities etc.

From a sales planning perspective, it's important you ask yourself some questions about your backstory so that you can put together information to enable you to do different forms of cross-channel storytelling as you progress. Having this ready as part of your sales tools will help you a lot.

- Why did you start the business?
- What gave you the idea?
- What is your working background? Is it linked to the business or a different background?
- Was there an event or something that triggered you starting the business?
- What makes you passionate about your business?
- What are some of the difficulties you have experienced?
- What drives you?
- What are you passionate about outside of the business?

- Is there an alignment between your personal story and your business story?

Unique Selling Points (USPs)

USP stands for unique selling point, and it essentially means the things that make your business different. What does it offer that makes it better than your competitors?

USPs could be all sorts of things from the specific experience and expertise of the founders through to a unique service that you offer that is way cheaper than similar services elsewhere, or a unique way in which you deliver services.

Ideally, I think you need to establish 3-4 USPs for business and the services it offers.

If you use these USPs effectively in content and when selling to people in the traditional way they can become a powerful tool in the salesperson's toolkit. Essentially, when it comes to making a sale, having strong USPs can help tip the balance and help a client to choose you over the competition.

For example, some of the USPs of my company, Brand Planning Ltd, are below. Brand Planning Ltd is a very small consultancy / agency, so some of its key USPs relate to my experience.

- I have 25 years' experience in the digital sector – that's a very long time and makes me one of the very early entrants into digital. It's a USP because very few consultants (especially in the local area in which I focus) are likely to have this level of experience.

- I have extensive experience in sales, traditional marketing, inbound marketing (SEO, PPC etc.), website development, content planning and writing, social selling and advertising. This is a very rare and powerful combination, meaning I can take a good strategic view of the whole picture and how it should fit together to maximise sales. This is a USP because very few people are likely to have this broad experience and skill set.

- I have a lot of very senior-level connections. This is a USP because it means I can help provide opportunities and introductions to my clients by utilising the power of the high-quality network I have built up over many years.

- I focus my services on sales. This is a USP locally as there are very few other consultants in the local area that specialise in sales. There are far more that specialise in marketing.

To devise your USPs it's important to first have completed other elements of the 10-point UniC sales planning process (or to be working on them at the same time) – because things like competitor analysis, a SWOT analysis, your brand values, service offering and several other elements will help work out your USPs and how to position them.

Product / Service Offering and Packages

Your Service Offering

To be able to sell services effectively, you need to have a clear idea of the range of services you are offering, and their features and benefits (i.e. what the intricacies of the services are and how these benefit your potential prospects – ideal clients).

For example, if you provide a copywriting service you could have 3–4 different services with different features and benefits:

Range of Services

- SEO-friendly blog service
- Storytelling article service
- Brochure writing service.

Example Features of Blog Service

The blog service features could be:

- Blogs of 1000 words
- Includes 2 hours of keyword research
- SEO-friendly.

Example Benefits of Blog Service

- Helps drive visitors from SEO
- Makes website more interesting for the user
- Can be repurposed for other use.

Whilst the storytelling article service and brochure writing service could have totally different features and benefits.

Using Features and Benefits to Sell Offline and Online

In terms of selling your service, you need to think about how the service will ease the potential purchaser's problems and benefit them.

To do this effectively you need to work out who your ideal prospects are and what their pain points are. Before you start selling, you can then collate a list of features and think of benefits of these features to match the potential pain points.

Then, when in a one-to-one sales situation you want to try and find out the prospect's actual difficulties and identify their needs. This is done through good questioning.

Once you know their pain points and needs you can start to match the potential benefits of your services to their needs (in your head) and start talking about the features of the most appropriate service and how this could help them.

When the conversation continues, you can then start to relay to the prospect how this service could really benefit them and reduce the current issues (pain points) they have.

Simplicity Sells

Similarly, the copy on your website should promote the features of your services and also outline how they may help your potential prospects (i.e. copy on the website should position the features and benefits and be written with the ideal prospect in mind). The idea being that the copy shows the visitor how your business could help them with the typical pain points they are likely to be suffering from.

I think one of the best ways to sell services is to keep things simple, so you can talk about the features and benefits very easily. Often for small businesses I have found the best way to do this is by creating simple packages.

There is so much involved in the actual sales process that I can't go into that in too much detail in this book. The main points to get across in this service offering section is that your services need to be positioned exceptionally well online so your potential prospects will see how they might benefit from them when reading your website copy.

Offline you need to have intricate knowledge of what the services consist of and how they can benefit the potential buyer.

You need to do the following:

- Gain an understanding of all the ins and outs of your services (features)
- Learn what they do (problems they solve – how they fix prospects' pain points)
- Work out benefits of the above point for the prospect, plus any additional benefits you can think of
- Keep things simple – simplicity sells
- Get the copy on your web pages written well (probably by specialists – sales copy is quite an art)
- Introducing easy-to-sell packages could be a great idea
- Have sales literature ready that can be sent out about the services
- Know your pricing and / or make it available to be seen if you want to (via your website and / or sales literature).

Elevator Pitches

An elevator pitch is a short pitch about you, your business, and the products and services you offer, and it can be used in all sorts of places.

An elevator pitch is one of the most important low-cost tools that you can add to your sales toolbox.

If you can create one initial elevator pitch as your base, and from this also create a few versions of alternative lengths, it should be one of the most powerful tools for your business.

In fact, after strong sales foundations have been developed, I think the three most powerful tools a business owner has, sales-wise, are as follows:

- Brand (including domain / brand messaging)
- Website (with info on your key services)
- Elevator pitch (which includes your USPs).

These three things alone, combined with a business owner (or lone salesperson) who knows how to sell and use these tools effectively should be enough for any small business to generate sufficient sales to take the business forward productively.

So, I just want to emphasise how very important I think it is sales-wise to plan, develop and learn how to deliver good elevator pitch(es) for your business.

How Long Should Elevator Pitches Be?

The typical length of an elevator pitch for networking events is 60 seconds.

Often, you will be asked to do a 60-second pitch, but sometimes events are short of time, so you are likely to need a 30-second version too.

You might get the opportunity to be the person in the spotlight and do a three-minute slot too. So, it's good to perfect this length of your elevator pitch as well.

Last, but not least, there is what I have named the 'coffee-table pitch'. This is just one or two very succinct sentences, no more than 15 seconds. This is a really good tool to pull out of the sales toolkit when someone comes up to you at a networking event and says, "So, tell me, what do you do?".

This often happens when you are by the drinks area, and that's why I call this the coffee-table pitch.

This really short version of your elevator pitch can be used in all sorts of other situations too when you're out and about, and get the opportunity to use elements of your pitch.

So, I suggest having three or four different versions of a short coffee-table pitch ready to use in different scenarios. If you use the questions below as a guide it will help you to create several different 15-second pitches that you can add to your sales toolkit.

- What do you do?
- How do you do it?
- How does what you do help other business owners?
- Why might people need your service?

By having a short 15-second pitch answering each of the above points in your sales toolkit, you can pull out the right pitch at the right time.

Where Are Elevator Pitches Used?

The most common place for an elevator pitch to be used is at networking events both online and offline. However, elevator pitches can also be used at the following places.

- **Local events** – you may get an opportunity to do a short elevator pitch in front of an audience at a local event.

- **Expos** – both local exhibitions and bigger ones are a great time to use your elevator pitch. If you are exhibiting on a stand, people will come and ask you what you do. You need a quick response that not only tells them what you do but explains why you do it well, and leaves them remembering you and wanting to find out more. A good elevator pitch is great for this.

  You can also use your elevator pitch when you visit other people's stands too. Once a two-way conversation gets started, it can become a bit like networking, so it is a great opportunity for you to use your pitch (or short sections of it).

- **At workshops** – a lot of workshop events give attendees a few minutes to introduce themselves before the workshop starts. This is another great opportunity to use your elevator pitch. The brilliant thing about workshops is that you're often sitting with like-minded people / prospects, yet it does not seem like a 'sales' environment.

  I think workshops are a great chance for business opportunities to arise (including sales opportunities), and having an elevator pitch ready is really advantageous.

Impromptu Elevator Pitches

- **Social events** – these can be another great opportunity to deliver your elevator pitch. You just have to do it in the right way, so you don't sound like you're pitching.

  It does take a bit of practice to adapt elevator pitches for situations like this. It starts with having a solid base pitch that you know inside out and taking one or two sentences from it to use at the right time.

  For example, when at a local event such as a quiz night, it can be a great time to meet other small business owners and let them know what you do.

- **Out and about** – if you get yourself so comfortable with the basis of your elevator pitch and can adapt it easily to say the right parts at the right time to the right people, then you can pretty much use it anywhere you want.

  For example, if you go to an indoor market, you could genuinely be browsing, but if you happen to get chatting to a stall owner that fits your prospect criteria, you can step into soft sales mode by using short sections of your elevator pitch. It really is about having the tools to hand (i.e. the elevator pitch) and the sales skill and communication skill to know when and how to use it.

How well your elevator pitch works for you does relate to how well the other elements of the sales foundations have been planned and developed. For example, having a clear idea of your target audience, a good website and sales material ready all help immensely in terms of sales being generated from you pitching your elevator pitch.

Tips About Elevator Pitches

One of the difficulties I hear people say about networking is that it's very time-consuming, and this is true. So, it can be difficult for some business owners to fit in as many networking events as they would like.

This is one very good reason why it's important to perfect your elevator pitch and elements of it in various time formats. That way, you can use it in all sorts of different scenarios, many of them just as you go about your day-to-day activities.

However, this requires great communication skills too, and this often requires some professional help. The value of investing in improving your communication skills by working with specialists can pay off immensely, as this can really help you improve your business from a sales perspective.

> So, knowing your elevator pitch, being able to adapt your elevator pitch for the right scenarios, and communicating your pitch effectively to the right people at the right time are all very important considerations.

Another good tip is knowing when not to pitch. Whilst I'm very pro using elements of your elevator pitch anytime, anywhere, you do need to be able to read people and the situation and know when it's an appropriate time to do this. If it's not an appropriate time, don't do it!

I'm certainly not suggesting that you push your pitch on people when they're not likely to want to hear it, but I am suggesting have it in mind and ready to use whenever it seems like a good chance to do so.

Judging when it's a good time and when it's not a good time to deliver parts of your elevator pitch is down to sales skill and communication skills, and this is something that can be learnt and taught, and gets easier with experience.

Business Cards

Another thing that I think you should do that good salespeople do is carry a few business cards with you wherever you go. You never know when you will get a great opportunity to pitch, so having a few business cards on you is helpful.

Personally, I find that business cards are easier than tech methods, as sometimes technology or connectivity plays up, or phone battery is low. When having a sales-related discussion, part of the key of doing it well is being concise, succinct and very together in the way that you deliver what you are saying. So, handing a business card over is a very quick and easy way to do things and the flow of conversation won't be at risk from tech hitches.

Making Inroads with Existing Clients with Your Pitch

When talking about elevator pitches, it's good to remember to use your pitch when you are doing work for bigger companies.

Often, bigger companies or charities have various decision-makers in different departments.

So, if you are providing a service to one department and happen to sit next to someone at lunch from another department, then this can be a great opportunity to make use of your elevator pitch.

You don't have to sell anything, incidentally. What you must do is start conversations, open up discussion, and be prepared to deliver one or two lines of your elevator pitch if you can. Just to steer the conversation towards a discussion about what you do. This way you could create another great connection and potential sales prospect for the future, just from having a conversation over lunch.

What Makes a Good Elevator Pitch?

So, what are the key things to include in an elevator pitch?

First and foremost, you need to think about it properly, because you want it to do a number of things.

- Introduce you and your business
- Tell people what you do
- Explain what makes your products / services better than others
- Gain attention
- Encourage a positive response
- Be memorable.

The point about explaining what makes you better than others is important as it's this point that is going to help you make an impact with your elevator pitch.

It doesn't have to be just one thing either. This is where knowing your values and your USPs is important because in the 60 seconds or 30 seconds you have available, you need to get across some USPs.

Doing this is what will make people sit up and listen to what you are saying and raise their interest. So, the better your planning of your values and your USPs, the stronger and more impactful your elevator pitches are likely to be.

I explain more about how to deliver your elevator pitch effectively on page 200.

Basic Keyword Planning

Basic keyword planning is another important foundational element of the 10-point UniC sales planning process.

I firmly believe that good use of keywords underpins long-term digital success, but deciding on a keyword strategy early on is something that is overlooked by so many businesses. I think it is because many small business owners associate keyword usage purely with SEO activity and do not realise how important it is for other areas of digital.

Often, small businesses assume that SEO activity is going to be way too expensive for them to begin with, and as a result, they make the mistake of failing to look at keyword usage at all.

This is unfortunate, because keywords are a fundamental part of so many elements of digital. If more businesses took time to think about their keyword strategy at the start-up stage, then I think this would help a lot of businesses achieve success with their digital activity more quickly. Whilst SEO can be an extremely good thing for many businesses to do, and can produce a great ROI, the entry costs are often far beyond the initial marketing budgets of start-ups or early-stage SMEs.

However, just because a company is not in the position to undertake full-blown ongoing SEO, this does not mean they should not undertake keyword research and keyword planning at the outset. These are fundamental processes that help develop a website, so it has strong foundations for SEO.

I think start-ups / small businesses should look at a keyword strategy as being one of the very first areas they invest some marketing budget into. In my opinion, keyword planning should be considered as early as possible – at the initial market research stage. It should then also be looked at on an ongoing basis for various areas of digital activity as the business progresses. The first of these is likely to be web development.

Keywords play a big part in all sorts of digital areas. Good keyword planning at the early stages of the sales planning and web development process will (a) help a website gain some SEO traction (if certain other areas of foundational SEO work are done at the outset); (b) help with future PPC and social media activity; and (c) help create a strong springboard for future SEO work to be applied, once the business is in a position to invest in ongoing SEO activity.

Some of the other areas of digital where keyword research and planning is important are outlined below.

- Competitor analysis
- Brand identity
- Social media profiles
- Directory listings
- Website content writing
- Internal search mechanisms – on websites
- Amazon and similar marketplaces
- Video and YouTube
- Social media posting
- PPC
- Blog planning and writing
- Local SEO
- LinkedIn articles

- Blogs on other sites
- PR.

Using Specialists for Keyword Research

Keyword planning is something that in theory anyone can do. However, I believe that good keyword planning is an art, much like SEO. This is because there are all sorts of things that must be taken into consideration when doing keyword research and planning.

Planning an SEO-based keyword strategy for a website build is a bit like a jigsaw – you need to be able to visualise the longer-term picture when you have hundreds of keywords (individual pieces in front of you) and you need to know what pieces to start with and what order to use the pieces – this is one reason why specialist help is so valuable.

Because keyword research forms the foundations on which much of the rest of your digital activity is built, it is extremely important to get this element right.

Whilst you may have to wait to do inbound marketing campaigns (due to budget constraints), ensuring that your website has strong foundations for inbound marketing growth should be a major consideration when having a website built. Keyword research plays a major part in this process.

An Introduction to Search Engine Optimisation

Search engine optimisation (SEO) is the art of helping businesses to achieve first-page listings on major search engines. SEO is a very complex area with lots of things that need to be done to make it work well. To achieve success in the search engines, ongoing monthly SEO work from a specialist SEO agency is highly likely to be required.

As a ballpark figure, it is likely to cost an SME upwards of £500 per month on an ongoing basis to use a specialist SEO agency. Often, you can be looking at £1000+ per month (it depends on the amount of work required and the sector etc.). Also, initial webwork which incorporates SEO foundation work is an integral component. The cost of this is estimated at £2000 or more (based on a 10-page website).

The expense is because SEO is complex and there is a lot of specialist planning and technical work involved, and SEO agencies that do things well have to charge a reasonable price for this work.

Sales Literature and Visuals (Graphics and Images)

Sales literature, graphics and images are three important things that you need to have in your sales toolkit as these will help you to make and close sales.

Sales Literature

If you have a good website, sales literature is less important than it used to be because you can direct people to your website for further information on what you do.

However, sales literature and materials are still important to enable you to sell effectively. I have listed on the next page some of the key things you are likely to need.

- Business cards
- Information on your services / packages to send out to people by email
- A rate card of all your services
- Sales terms and conditions
- Additional info to send out to people who are interested – PDFs etc. with more info than is on your website
- Branded sales proposal templates
- Possibly a pull-up banner for local expos
- Maybe some branded products for local expos
- Flyers to hand out at some networking events
- A pitch deck – a presentation about your business and what you do that is approx. 30 minutes in length (and could easily be made longer or shorter) for you to use for presentations.

Graphics

Ideally you will require a set of branded graphics to use on social media.

This will include things like your personal and business page profile banners for LinkedIn and maybe a basic set of graphics for posts.

You will also need your logo – so you can send this to people when you do different forms of PR, editorial etc.

Images

You need a great headshot for LinkedIn – this is important as it makes a positive impact on encouraging people to warm to you / your profile, which makes connecting and striking up conversations easier.

One great set of professional photos – a starter set showing you in different outfits and surroundings (i.e. some outside and some inside) – is recommended for use across your website, your sales and marketing material, and in PR etc.

With graphics and photos there are some fantastic professionals in local areas who charge reasonable rates, and I think it is very advisable to use professionals. Having professional photos taken makes a very positive impact on first impressions. It is also likely to help your confidence when it comes to making sales

Using a specialist makes things look more professional in my opinion, and that adds a great deal of value from a sales and a marketing perspective.

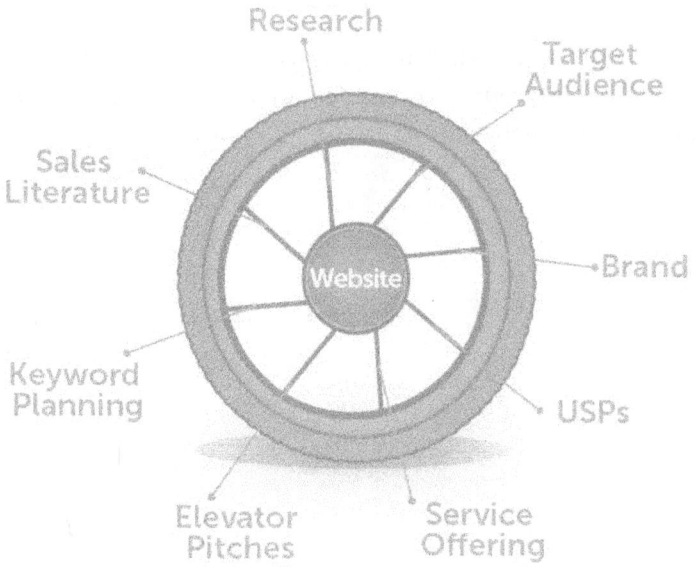

CHAPTER 14:

Element 4: The Sales Toolkit

Below is a list of all the key things that I think a small business needs to have in their sales toolkit before they start spending too much time or money on marketing.

Brand and digital assessment	Domain name
Tagline	Logo
Sales-focused SWOT analysis	Competitor analysis
Sales skills (i.e. basic training)	Sales strategy
6 x ideal decision-maker overviews	Overview of niche specialism
Service-offering overview	Packages overview
List of features and benefits	Sales objectives and KPIs
USP planning	Sales literature / materials
List of potential objections and responses	Keyword research – 10 terms – so any future SEO / PPC planning / activity has keyword guidelines
Sales messaging (planning)	Some recommendations / testimonials
Networking planning	Basic website
Elevator pitch – coffee table	Brand values and brand story
Elevator pitch – 3 more short versions	Sales prospects – starter pipeline
Elevator pitch – 30 seconds	List of client pain points
Elevator pitch – 60 seconds	'About Us' web page
Elevator pitch – 3 minutes	LinkedIn profile
Target market / prospect breakdown	LinkedIn business page
Images	Basic LinkedIn sales strategy and KPIs
Graphics	Keynote presentation

Sales Pipeline

One thing that all good salespeople usually do is maintain a sales pipeline. By sales pipeline, I mean they build a list on an ongoing basis of potential prospects and continue to add to and update the list on an ongoing basis.

This is something that experienced salespeople know they must do come rain or shine as it is the continual growth of this pipeline that keeps sales flowing.

When prospects first get put on the list they will simply be at a stage where the salesperson has identified them as good prospects that meet their target criteria. At this point, the prospects would be classed as what is commonly known as a 'cold lead'.

As time progresses, and the salesperson has discussions, and then meetings with the prospect, the prospect will turn from being a cold lead into a warmer lead until eventually they become a hot prospect, and, in an ideal world, turn into a sale.

Some will turn into sales, some will just stay in the pipeline for ages, and some will turn back to be very cold until they need to be removed as they are clearly not going to become a sale.

How you manage your sales pipeline will depend on various things and this topic is a much more complex area of discussion. There are things that need to be considered such as what systems to use to store information, so this overview is just to provide insight about the purpose of a sales pipeline, not the technicalities or legalities.

The main point I want to make is that the pipeline work needs to be continual through busy times too as this is how most good salespeople keep sales flowing. It is also what helps you from having too many peaks and troughs.

Top 10 Prospects

To begin with, many small business owners may not have a sales pipeline, so I suggest to my clients that a top 10 prospect list is a good idea.

This means identifying 10 ideal prospects for the future. It just requires the name of the companies, the sector they are in and why they are a good fit.

This very basic list can become the starting point to build a future sales pipeline.

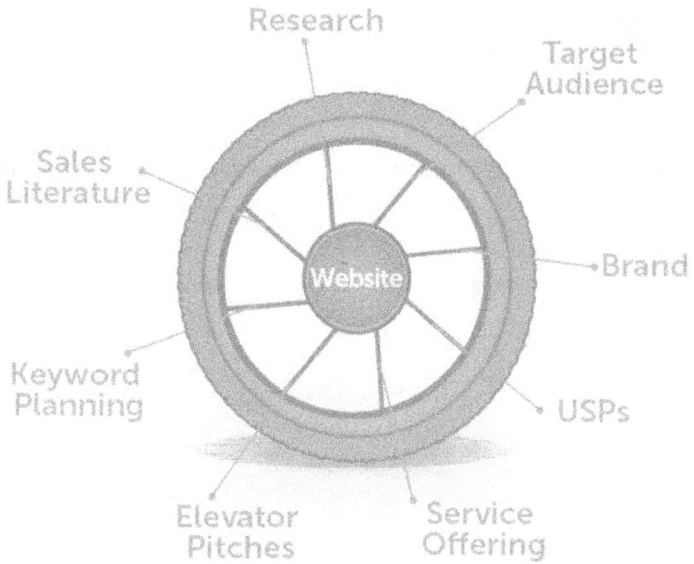

Research
Target Audience
Sales Literature
Website
Brand
Keyword Planning
USPs
Elevator Pitches
Service Offering

CHAPTER 15:

Element 5: Networking

The Importance of Networking

Business networking is one of the best and cheapest ways to make sales. Get this right and it should be one of the key things that helps kickstart the cyclical approach to sales that I referred to in the early chapters of the book.

There is lots you can learn about improving networking skills. The list on page 198 will help you with some tips about how to network more effectively when you are at networking events.

However, it's very important to remember that successful networking is not just about what you do on the day at the event. It's about what you do before and after the event. Without getting the before and after bits right, what you do at the event is somewhat pointless! So, it's worth noting that good work before and after you attend networking events is of paramount importance.

As far as the UniC sales planning process is concerned, I'd go as far as suggesting that networking could be compared to the pedals that are required to make the sales planning wheel start to go round. It's that important! And for so many different reasons!

Online or Offline Networking?

There are advantages and disadvantages of both online and offline networking. Personally, I would choose in-person networking above online networking if I had to make a choice as I think it is a far better activity from a sales perspective for many reasons.

In addition, I like to get out and see people in person. I think offline networking has additional benefits for business owners that revolve around getting away from the screen, having in-person interaction with others and building strong business relationships.

However, I do combine my networking activities, and I do both offline and online networking regularly.

I am aware that online networking can be a better option for some people though, and whilst I would always encourage SMEs to do a mix of both, if possible, I have listed some advantages that online networking can offer people.

- **Time-saving** – online networking saves so much travel time and you can go to a great event for an hour or two without having to travel anywhere.
- **Wide choice** – there is a massive choice of online events to go to – more so than offline as you often don't have to consider location. So, it is a great way to get to more events where your target prospects may be.

- **Introvert-friendly** – for those people that really don't like the idea of offline networking and / or for those who do, but who may be having a bad day (e.g. not feeling like a social butterfly) then online can sometimes be an easier way to network. It gives you the opportunity to still meet people, but you have the option of remaining more behind the screen (as it were).
- **Stepping stone** – online networking can potentially be a great stepping stone to get those who are less confident with networking used to it and it can ease you in. Some groups are so friendly and do both online and offline events. So, you can potentially start with online, get to know regular attendees, and then move on to some of the offline events with the same group when you are ready.

What If You Dislike the Idea of Any Type of Networking?

Some people steer clear of networking altogether because it fills them with dread. The idea of walking into a room full of strangers and making polite conversation and / or the thought of doing an elevator pitch might make them incredibly anxious.

If you are one of these people, whatever I say here will probably not allay those fears. However, I think you will be missing out massively from a sales perspective if you don't go networking. I also believe that by working with the right specialists you should be able to overcome these fears.

I'd suggest trying this first, but if you don't feel you can, then it may be worth considering working alongside someone who can help network on behalf of your business.

Alternatively, maybe you could try online networking first. This could potentially give you the opportunity to get used to a group without having to get too involved.

Helping people get over networking confidence issues and network more effectively is a service I provide (at the time of writing this book).

I offer in-person group sessions and sessions on a one-to-one basis – so, if you are based in or around London and think you may be interested in finding out more about this then more info can be found at brandplanning.co.uk/b2b-networking

Before You Start Networking

Going through the foundational elements section from the 10-point UniC sales planning process will enable you to put in place all the fundamental things you need to start networking effectively. These include:

- target audience knowledge
- unique selling points knowledge
- elevator pitch preparation (several versions)
- sales materials – to send out to people that may be interested in knowing more.

In addition, it helps immensely to have an initial website in place when you go networking (even if it is very small) and / or a great LinkedIn page that relays your core business information / service info.

Also, you need to take your networking activity very seriously for it to be very effective from a sales perspective. It's not something you can do half-heartedly if you want it to be very successful.

Essentially, like most of the things I talk about in this book that relate to sales, you need to be strategic in your networking approach and activity to produce the best results.

One thing that should help get you started, is for you to test out the networking scene by going to a selection of different events and trying them out. This should enable you to work out which ones are likely to be the best ones for you to attend regularly.

Something to bear in mind is that one thing that is important with networking is consistency. By this I mean it is better to go to some of the same events (held monthly) than it is to keep going to different events.

However, you only have so much time to network, so it helps to be very selective in your approach. How you select the right networking events to attend should circle around knowing your target audience, your values and what you want to achieve from your networking activity.

Benefits of Going to the Same Networking Events Regularly

Ideally, you want to find events that are most likely to help to get you in front of your target audience in one way or another. Alternatively, the events you choose could have other benefits such as enabling you to build strong relationships with well-established business owners in your local area, as these people can be great to talk to and learn from, plus they can potentially help open doors.

The reason for finding ones to go to regularly is because this helps you start to build up strong business relationships with other small business owners that go regularly too. This has value for so many reasons, as outlined below.

- These people will become your supporters on social media.
- They should help you spread the word of what you do on social media.
- They should help you find out about other events.
- They will be people you can share your business struggles with and be open with. Sharing challenges with others in a similar situation is a great way to alleviate concerns and find ways to do things more productively.
- Over time, some of these people may also become friends. Having friends in business that you know, like and trust can help make business so much easier.

Networking regularly is so important, and I always think it helps to be ahead of the game with networking. This means planning your networking diary way ahead of time. I think it is good to do this a month in advance if you can.

This way, you can then fit all your actual sales meetings and supplier meetings around your networking diary. At times, networking events will have to fall by the wayside if a client meeting comes up that is more pressing. However, in my experience, with good organisation and planning ahead of time, this rarely happens.

Your wardrobe is another important consideration that should be thought about before you go to networking events. Whilst this may sound like a silly thing, it's not. First impressions count for a lot, so if you are going to be doing a lot of meetings and networking events then make sure that you've kitted out your wardrobe so that you look the part.

Why Knowing What Type of Connections You Want is So Important

It helps to have a clear idea of the type of people you want to connect with before you go to networking events. These are likely to include the following.

- **Ideal prospects** – you should have a clear idea of who your ideal prospects are from the target audience work you will have done as part of the early 10-point planning work. This is important because you only have limited time to go to networking events. Also, when you're at the networking events, the time you have to meet different people is likely to whizz by. Therefore, knowing your target prospect helps immensely as it enables you to be selective and specifically approach people that fit your criteria.

- **People in similar industries to either you or your ideal prospects** – connecting with people from similar industries is usually a good idea in my view for several reasons. You may be able to work on projects together for example, or they may be able to introduce you to people that could be good connections, or they may pass work to you when they can't handle it.

- **Potential suppliers (i.e. people whose services you might want to use one day)** – it's always good to be forward-thinking in what you might need for your business in the future and building up potential supplier contacts is a good idea for this reason. However, once connected, these contacts may also be able to refer people to you in the future.

- **Heavy business networkers or well-connected people in the local community** – I am one of these myself, and it's always good to look out for these types of people as they are the ones that could introduce you to many others and potentially open doors.

- **People you think you might be able to help** – why? Because if you help your network with introductions, it might get paid back. Regardless of whether it gets paid back or not, it's a nice thing to do if you are working in a local community.

After Networking Events

Soon after you have been to a networking event, I think it's a really good idea to sit down and make some mental notes to yourself about who you met and spoke to. Take time to really think about this so that you install in your own memory details of who you spoke to, what their names were, what they looked like and some basic things you spoke about.

This really helps for future networking. It's extremely powerful to be able to meet somebody once and then the second time you meet them instantly remember their name and things about them. People notice this and it helps reignite conversations at the next meeting.

Following Up

Sadly, too many people waste time going to networking events because they do not follow up afterwards. If you don't follow up, it totally defeats the object of going in the first place.

Sales are not generally done at networking events themselves. In fact, I'd encourage you not to sell at events apart from the short time in which you do your elevator pitch.

> Going to networking events should not be about selling there and then. Instead, it should be about making new connections, building rapport with people and explaining briefly what you do (as and when appropriate). With new contacts you meet it should be about briefly finding out what these people do too. It should also be about regularly catching up and talking about business with existing contacts.

As far as I am concerned, the primary purpose of networking is to meet people briefly and then to either connect and / or continue discussions with them afterwards. This starts with the first follow-up you do, which should happen a day or two after the event — so you need to be mindful of this and put time aside for your follow-up work.

Following up after the event is something that is so important. What I mean by this is connecting with the people you have met for the first time that you think it could be worth maintaining a relationship with (for several business-related reasons).

This does not just have to be because you think they could be a good prospect either. It could be because they could potentially be a good supplier for you in the future, or they could just be a good local contact that you think it is going to be worth continuing building a relationship with.

These days, I think the initial follow-up is usually best done via LinkedIn – first as a connection request and, where relevant, as a direct message to continue discussions with a view to arranging a one-to-one meeting.

With many contacts it is good enough to initially just take the follow-up to the point of connecting with each other on LinkedIn – knowing that maybe a meeting might happen at another time in the future.

With a few contacts (usually those that you had more in-depth and lengthy chats with at the networking event), when you do the follow-up you can take the discussion further and try to arrange to meet over a coffee or do a one-to-one video call to find out more about what you both do. In my mind this should not be viewed as the starting point for the traditional sales process though – but instead, quite literally, a general initial intro / discussion meeting.

If during this first meeting it then becomes apparent that there is scope for the contact to become a good potential prospect, then this is where I'd suggest it would be beneficial to try to get a secondary meeting and / or the go-ahead to send follow-up information.

In my opinion, it is the point at which the contact accepts either of the two things above that in your mind they should change from being a cold prospect to a slightly warmer prospect that may have genuine interest in your products / services.

The Bridge Between Networking Events and Social Selling

LinkedIn is the perfect channel to connect with people after a networking event. It's here you can start to build a far deeper connection and relationship with contacts and maybe arrange a meeting or video call. Alternatively, you can just start commenting on your new connection's posts.

The bridge between networking and social selling on LinkedIn is one that not enough small business owners seem to know about or use, but it is incredibly powerful.

If you continue strengthening the relationship with contacts (potential prospects) that you initially met at online or offline networking via communication on LinkedIn, these prospects quickly start to become warmer prospects.

It helps them to start to know, like and trust you more. Then, when they are ready, it should be easier to arrange meetings and start moving things forward down the traditional sales-process route. This is because they already know, like and trust you. Part of the reason for this is because they become used to seeing you on social media, but it's more than that. It's because there was a human connection at a networking event earlier on in the relationship and, in my mind, nothing beats human contact as far as sales is concerned (even if the initial contact is by video call).

So, combining networking and using LinkedIn effectively as a social selling tool to strengthen the relationship initially made at networking is, in my mind, one of the best ways for small businesses to start to make sales.

Its success, however, is highly dependent on the following:

- The pre-networking fundamentals being in place
- Networking skills being used effectively at events
- The availability of sales material (e.g. PDFs, rate cards)
- A good website.

This is because it is the things above that can help tip the balance between someone having an interest in wanting to arrange a meeting with you, or not.

Arranging Meetings Through Social Selling

Social selling is a specific type of sales and one that there is a lot to learn about. I think for best results it sits alongside (and works in conjunction with) both networking and account-based marketing (ABM).

ABM is essentially a very targeted form of marketing, which I think is more like sales. Essentially, it's about being strategic with how you approach and deliver sales / marketing messages / communication to a defined and highly targeted audience.

After meeting people at networking events, if they fit your ideal prospect criteria, the goal should be to get to the point of a one-to-one meeting. This may not be possible straight away though. So, the combination of appearing regularly at events that these people go to (regular networking) and social selling (commenting on their posts, direct messages etc.) is somewhat of a two-pronged approach.

Over time, if done well, this two-pronged approach should get you seen by the prospect more regularly so that you are front of mind when they are thinking of using your type of service. Ultimately this continual contact should progress to a meeting at some point.

This could however take many months, if not years to happen. It's this slow but sure method of strengthening relationships that is one of the reasons why consultancy-style sales are so good when they do come in – but also why they take a long time to secure. The length of time they can take to turn is also why it's so important to have a sales pipeline that is constantly being added to and nurtured.

I can't go into too much detail about social selling or account-based marketing in this book as they are complex areas and there are other good books about these subjects. A list of these can be found on the Sales Before Marketing website at salesbeforemarketing.com/marketing-books

I will, however, explain a bit more about social selling on page 227.

Networking Tips – for During Events

Business networking can be one of the best ways for small businesses to gain new prospects / clients but there is an art to networking effectively.

Overleaf are just a few tips – things that I think make the process more productive.

- Arrive 10 minutes early wherever possible.
- Know who your ideal type of prospects are before you go, so you can pick out the best people to have conversations with at the event.
- Smiling goes a long way – a good smile breaks the ice and opens doors to conversation.
- First impressions count for a lot – so dress well.
- Understanding body language of others helps.
- Your own body language is important – don't be too closed.
- Listen intently to others. Less talking and more listening.
- Ask open questions – what, when, where, why, who?
- Encourage people to talk – keep conversation going by asking more open questions.
- Pull other people into conversations if appropriate, if people are on their own.
- Have a good elevator pitch ready; ideally 2 or 3 of different style and length – this is very important!
- Do your elevator pitch as well as you can and make a note to yourself of mistakes you could improve on.
- Know the features and benefits of your product / service offering so if appropriate you can drop points into the conversation.
- Don't sell heavily though! Networking is not the time to do this – the objective should be to build relationships and get agreement to follow up.
- Keep up on current affairs and / or general things of interest so you can keep conversation flowing if it dries up – no-one wants long silences when networking.
- Don't invade people's personal space – leave a reasonable distance between yourself and who you are talking to.
- Holding a cup of drink on a saucer in one hand, food in the other, and trying to eat and drink whilst networking is a recipe for disaster – don't do all 3 at the same time!
- Approach at least 2–3 people who look like they may fit your ideal prospect criteria and try to talk to them.

- Exchange business cards with people you want to connect with.
- Agree to connect afterwards on LinkedIn.

Networking Planning and KPIs

- Prioritise networking over and above admin and client work that can be done at other times.
- Attend at least 4 networking events each month (ideally 8–12).
- Choose 2–3 groups to regularly attend monthly and do ad-hoc events.
- Say a brief hello and have a 60-second chat with as many people as you can.
- Try and have at least 1–2 longer chats with people of interest.
- Perfect your 60-second elevator pitch – keep practising it between events.
- Have general literature and / or a LinkedIn business page ready to send to people that show any interest.
- Arrange at least one meeting as a result of each networking event.
- Spend 1 hour per week (minimum) reconnecting with people you met last week / month at networking events.
- Put another 1 hour a week aside to message existing networking contacts in your network.
- Start commenting on new posts and sharing posts from new contacts made.

Delivering Your Elevator Pitch So it Makes a Positive Impact

Good elevator pitch delivery can open all sorts of doors, sales-wise.

It may seem like a lot, but 60 seconds is not actually very long to deliver all the necessary information from your elevator pitch well; 30 seconds is even less time, so you really need to practise getting the delivery of your elevator pitch right once you have written the pitch.

Before you deliver an elevator pitch it's worth remembering the point I made at the beginning of the book about how I liken it to a footballer about to score a goal.

Just like a footballer, when you step on to the pitch, I think you should do the following:

- Know your target.
- Focus on the target and how you are going to score.
- Aim for a great delivery.
- Put your weight behind it.
- Kick it right across the field (or audience).
- Put great spin on it.
- And score with a goal they won't forget – i.e. make it memorable.

The first thing you need to do is introduce yourself and your business, which is easy enough. How you deliver this information is pivotal though.

People make decisions very quickly on first impressions as to whether they warm to somebody. So, the first impression you make with this part of your elevator pitch can make or break how the rest of the pitch goes and the response you're likely to get.

In the networking scenario, the following things help a lot with this.

- Dress well and look the part.
- Stand up, stand tall and stand with confidence.
- Stay open with your body language, don't cross your arms and use your hands – be animated.
- Look around the room, make eye contact with a few people as you deliver the opening line. Ideally these people should be ones you have already identified as target prospects.
- Smile, with your mouth and with your eyes.
- Deliver the words confidently and show that you have passion about your business.
- Speak clearly and positively throughout.
- Encourage people to contact you once you have come to the end.
- Make sure you keep smiling at the end.
- Look around the room and gain more eye contact as you repeat your name, your company and web address at the end.

There is a lot to remember about delivering a good elevator pitch, but I always think it's like acting. You need to know your lines, deliver them incredibly well and adapt to situations when on stage (i.e. sometimes you need to improvise a bit).

When elevator pitches are delivered extremely well, they can be very impactful, and I believe good elevator pitch delivery can be one of the best ways to gain interest from potential prospects.

Choose Your Seat Carefully

There are a few other tips that I have regarding the delivery of elevator pitches.

The first good tip is not to sit near the host. Sit further away. That way you won't be likely to go first, and it gives you a chance to hear lots of other people's pitches.

If you know clearly who your target audience is (which you should do from doing the sales planning foundation element) then the time spent listening to other people's pitches is a golden time from a sales perspective.

This is because this time enables you to quickly identify the people in the room that could be good potential prospects before you pitch. Then, when you come to pitch you can direct your eye contact, your body language and smile towards these people specifically to help gain their interest. It's a perfect opportunity to reel in your ideal client. If you become good at delivering elevator pitches you can even tailor your pitch with them in mind by mentioning their company sector or similar things to heighten their attention and interest.

Recap on Elevator Pitches

So, to summarise.

Elevator pitches are one of the most important sales tools you will have, so you need to get used to using them if you want to make more sales.

I suggest starting by creating a 60-second pitch and adapting this so it is decreased and expanded until eventually you have the following:

- 15-second coffee-table pitch
- 15-second micro pitches (x 3) as outlined on page 168
- 30-second pitch
- 60-second pitch
- 3-minute pitch
- 15-minute pitch / mini-presentation.

Pitching At Online Networking Events

When using elevator pitches at online networking events, often they will only be 30 seconds and it's harder to use body language which I think makes it more difficult from a sales perspective.

So, I think with online networking, be as clear as possible and keep your pitch simple and to the point. Also, with this type of networking I think your primary objective should be for your pitch to help you make connections with the right people via LinkedIn very shortly after the event, so they remember you. So, it helps to put 30 minutes aside after the event to do immediate follow-ups.

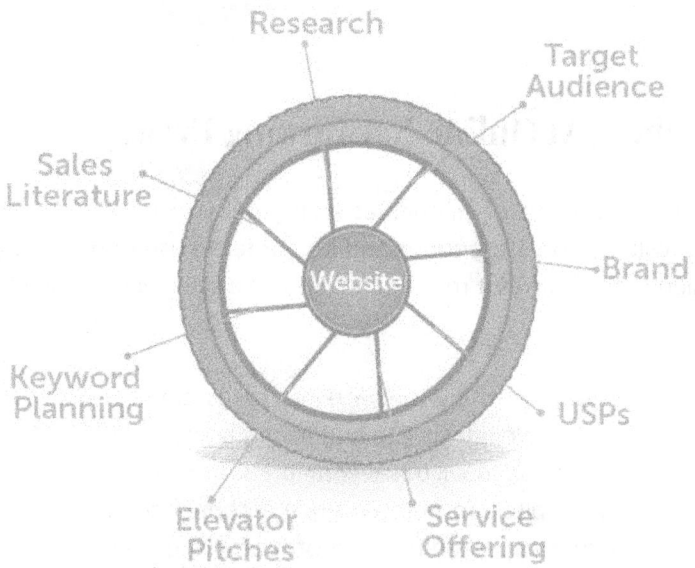

CHAPTER 16:

Element 6: Understanding the Sales Process and Learning How to Sell

To sell effectively you need to have some experience of the following areas, and if you don't have experience, I think you should either try and learn more about some of these areas or work with specialists.

- Traditional sales experience
- Digital marketing experience
- Networking experience / confidence
- Digital development experience – e.g. website development
- Social selling experience.

Before I explain more about how to sell, I thought it would be a good idea to outline some of the typical problems small business owners experience on the sales side with some quick tips from me on how to overcome these issues.

Typical Sales-related Problems

I've listed some sales-related issues that small business owners often experience below. These are very real problems that a lot of small business owners encounter regularly. The way to get over these is generally to have a better understanding of sales planning and how to sell.

No direction. Often small business owners don't know what direction to take but are bursting with ideas. This can result in them trying to do too many things at once, which is not beneficial for sales activity.

This issue can usually be resolved through good sales planning to establish a strong sales focus and more clarity on direction.

A lack of belief in products / services. Often, people seem to lack confidence in all sorts of areas related to sales because they don't believe in what they're selling.

One reason for this is because they don't have a clear idea of what it is they are actually selling – it's all a bit vague. By following the 10-point UniC sales planning process this problem can be easily solved, as gaining an in-depth understanding of what you are selling and who you want to sell to are key elements of building strong sales foundations.

A lack of confidence. Sometimes, confidence issues with sales are not to do with what is being sold, but more about how it is being sold. I often find that people lack confidence in their own ability to pitch the products and services that they are selling.

Essentially, whilst they have decided to act as the main salesperson for their business, they don't know how to act as the main salesperson, and they lack confidence in doing so.

This can be easily overcome by some basic sales training, including networking skills.

Concern about where the next sale will come from. Often, small business owners make the mistake of not selling during busy times. This leaves them without a sales pipeline to fall back on when it gets quiet. This leads to real concern for the business owner because they don't have a clear idea of where they are going to find their next sale.

They don't know who to contact first, or where to go, or what to do to bring new clients on quickly, and this leaves them going round in circles feeling concerned about the whole issue of sales.

Learning how to develop and build a strong sales pipeline will overcome this issue.

Confusion about what to do to improve things. I often find that people are confused about how to improve things. Because they have not been through a sales planning process and / or been taught how to sell effectively, they don't know where to start to improve things and that just leaves them with a sense of confusion.

Again, sales planning is a simple answer that will help rectify this.

Worry that sales are too slow coming in or that they won't come in at all.

In my mind this is just time wasted. Worrying about sales not coming in won't make them come in. Planning how to make sales and doing networking etc. is what will make them come in, and this is one reason why sales planning is so important.

Desperation. Sometimes, people feel real panic if they suddenly lose a big client or feel like they have hit a brick wall, sales-wise. I think they panic because they can't see a way forward. Suddenly, to them, losing the client spirals into something much bigger. It quickly becomes much more than losing one sale in their mind. Instead, it sparks off a whole load of worry and desperation about all sorts of things – e.g. a fear about paying bills, concern about job security, a feeling of inadequacy.

I think building a good network of other business owners and talking to people along the way about concerns you have can help when problems like this arise. There are other things you can do as well, like ensuring your business is not overly reliant on particular clients (i.e. spread the load). Also, the whole sales planning process should help things from getting to this stage.

A sense of inadequacy. When others boast how well they're doing at sales it can be easy for small business owners to feel downhearted and inadequate. I think this happens a lot more than it used to because people read posts from others on social media who claim to be doing brilliantly.

My answer to this is simple – don't listen to the noise and stay on your own path.

We have different ways of doing things and different objectives to achieve. Personally, I think a lot of what is shared on social media with people boasting about high-value or high-volume sales is often smoke and mirrors anyway. Just because someone says they have made thousands of pounds worth of sales provides no indication of how they did it, what their costs were, what the profit margin is, or how well their business is doing, so it's rather meaningless anyway.

A sense of defeat / failure. At times during my sales career I've felt like gaining new business seems like walking uphill through treacle, and I see this situation with other small business owners regularly.

At times like this I've always reverted to my early sales lessons and that's why it's so important to remember the point I made in Chapter 2 of this book about every 'No' you receive taking you one step closer to a 'Yes'.

Sales, by its sheer nature, is full of rejections and that's why it's also important to remember sales is a numbers game. The more people you pitch to, the more likely you are to make a sale. But also remember my caveat with this – that whilst numbers are important, it's quality over quantity that counts.

Stress from keeping quiet and letting sales worries build up internally.

This is one of the biggest concerns I have for small business owners. Making sales can be extremely hard and pressurised, but if you don't communicate with others, it can be a lot harder.

Letting stress build up is one of the things that can lead to a potential burnout / breakdown and so I think it's incredibly important to do whatever you can to avoid that. Mixing in circles with other business owners can really help and it's one of the key reasons that networking regularly and consistently can be so beneficial.

There are also a lot of groups and organisations that can help with stress-related issues, mental health and wellbeing, and there is a list of these on the Brand Planning Ltd website at brandplanning.co.uk/wellbeing

Points to Remember About Making Sales

Most good salespeople experience some / all of the points I have mentioned regularly throughout their careers. However, unlike many business owners they have the sales training, the team and the tools to help them overcome these things.

The team, training and tools help them learn how to have a salesperson's mindset, and so I thought it would be a good point to list some of the typical things experienced salespeople know.

10 Things Experienced Salespeople Know

1. **Seasonality can impact sales** – for example, August and December are widely seen as being difficult months, sales-wise, due to holidays. They are a great time for sales planning though, so working your activity around seasonality can be very beneficial. In the downtime, spend more time planning what you will do sales-wise, as you won't get much time for planning in peak networking / sales season (I'd say this is generally September–November and mid-January–May / June).

2. **Sales results can be like waiting for a bus** – you can put loads of time in and see none and then 3 arrive in a row. So, be patient and don't get downhearted if you have to wait a while!

3. **A deal is not done until it's signed on the dotted line (as it were)** – don't rely on sales that have not landed yet. This will reduce disappointment.

4. **Keep on building the sales pipeline** – the more potential there is in the pot, the more likelihood of something coming in.

5. **Keep selling when you're busy** – this may mean at times you have to work hard to manage servicing clients and

selling to new clients, but it should help avoid the peaks and troughs.

6. **Always be ready to step into sales mode** – you never know where your next sale will come from.

7. **Ask for referrals** – it's OK to ask clients to remember to refer others to you if they like the service they've received.

8. **Keep on chasing prospects** – it takes many points of contact for a sale to be made, and a lot of people give up too soon. Just be careful not to be overeager. Timing matters – you want to keep chasing if someone has shown an interest, but leave sufficient time in between each contact you do have – often weeks or months.

9. **Move on once a proposal has been sent out** – don't sit around waiting to hear; move on to the next prospect. Remember, it's a numbers game.

10. **Don't give up at ghosting** – if someone blanks you it doesn't mean they are not interested – they may just not be interested right now. Ghosting is a bit rude I think – a quick email doesn't take a moment – but business is full of different things going on. People are busy, things happen, things change, things get in the way, people may want to do it but can't and don't know how to say so – a whole load of things could be the reason. So, I think if you keep getting ghosted, leave it a while but don't leave it for good – still chase up again later down the line.

Tips When Experiencing Sales Concerns

Try not to get overwhelmed or too stressed – your mental health matters most and stress won't help sales come in.

Take a step back and give yourself thinking / planning time, away from the noise.

Take the quiet time to have a rest, look after your wellbeing, and gain strength.

Ignore what others do and focus on your business and what you can do to improve sales.

Remember, a lot of good salespeople will have had professional training because there's a lot to learn and there's an art to doing sales well. This is why it could prove very helpful to work with specialists on the sales side – to devise the strategy and provide you with training on how to sell.

The important things to do are to have strong sales foundations, have a good sales strategy, and keep building a solid sales pipeline whilst you wait for the sales to arrive.

How to Sell

In my opinion, the answer to this, first and foremost, is to go back to basics!

- Ensure that bullet points 1–3 of the 10-point UniC sales planning process have been done – including all 8 points of the foundations work, as it is this work that will give you the platform to sell effectively.

- You also need to go through points of the traditional sales process on page 81 and 82 to remind yourself of the key things that you need to think about when you get to the point of making sales.

- You should also find the 10 points on the next page helpful as they outline some of the key things you should be doing as you embark on ongoing sales activity.

1. Get in front of the right target audience as often as possible, either by putting yourself in front of them via networking, workshops, direct sales, social selling etc. or getting them to come to you – this can take many forms, such as social media marketing, inbound marketing (e.g. SEO, PPC, digital PR) and local advertising / promotional activity.
2. Build and nurture a prospect list and communicate with potential future prospects in various ways.
3. Build and nurture relationships with your potential referrers (your network).
4. Have all the tools ready to be responsive to warm leads / enquiries and quickly provide good info to warm leads.
5. Do a good job – i.e. provide a quality service.
6. Provide great customer care.
7. Get good feedback from clients.
8. Spread the word of the good feedback and encourage others to spread the word too.
9. Nurture the relationship with existing clients and upsell.
10. Build your brand awareness – thought-leadership pieces etc.

Using Questioning Techniques to Establish Needs and Listen to Answers

'Questioning words' are an extremely important part of good sales activity because these words help the sales process in lots of different ways.

Using questioning words effectively can be incredibly powerful when making sales and retaining clients.

What? Which? When? Where? Who? Why? and How? are good examples of questioning words. Using these words enables you to ask what are known as 'open questions'.

There is a primary reason why using these questioning words is important. It's because they encourage an answer that is not a 'Yes' or 'No'. This allows conversation to flow, and by asking a string of open questions it enables you to listen to the answers and start building a picture of the prospect, their situation and ideally their needs.

Questioning words are very useful in sales for other reasons too.

- **Planning** – they help you plan sales and marketing strategies more effectively by encouraging you to ask yourself important planning questions.

- **Networking** – they help you at business networking events by enabling you to start conversations and keep conversations flowing by asking questions.

- **Sales meetings** – they help you open sales meetings, build trust, and run good meetings.

- **Closing sales** – they can also help you close sales effectively.

- **Client retention** – they help you to provide good ongoing customer / client care and upsell where appropriate.

- **Monitoring sales and marketing results** – they help you monitor your own sales and marketing achievements by assisting you to question areas of activity and results achieved.

When it comes to sales, SME owners who learn to use questioning words effectively and listen to the answers are likely to have far more success than those who don't.

I cannot teach you more about how to sell in this book as I don't have enough pages to do so. However, there are lots of good sales books and websites around, and a list of these are on the Sales Before Marketing website – salesbeforemarketing.com/sales-books

At the time of writing this book, I also provide in-person group workshops in South London to help people improve sales skills.

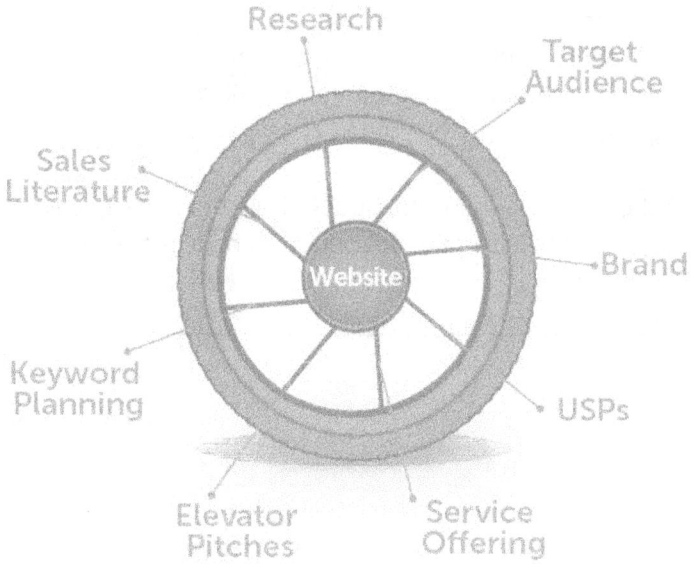

Research

Target
Audience

Sales
Literature

Website

Brand

Keyword
Planning

USPs

Elevator
Pitches

Service
Offering

CHAPTER 17

Element 7: Overarching Sales Strategy / A Hybrid Approach

The Hybrid Approach

Once the foundations and a sales plan are in place, a hybrid approach to low-cost sales and marketing (online and offline) should be the next step before you start spending too much on digital marketing activity.

By a hybrid approach, I mean combining online and offline sales, marketing and promotional activity to generate sales.

For small B2B businesses with low budgets, I think a mix of offline and online sales / marketing activity, with heavy emphasis on networking, social media marketing, social selling, local promotion and PR is usually the best approach in the early years. If carried out effectively, this low-cost hybrid approach should generate enough sales to help create a budget for different forms of digital marketing activity to start taking place.

Once sales start to be made, the first area that I think budget from initial sales should be applied to is the development of a professionally built website. I explain this in depth in Chapter 20 but, to summarise, the reason is because a good website is usually required for various other forms of digital marketing to be successful (including all forms of inbound marketing).

Know, Like and Trust

There is a saying that people buy people. My extensive experience in sales tells me this is true, and it's down to the know, like and trust words that we often hear.

People like to know who they are buying from, and they need to warm to them, and trust what they are being sold is good quality. This can to a certain degree work online (which is one big reason why a good website is so important) but it often works best offline or through a hybrid approach to sales.

I think for small businesses, networking is usually just as important for sales success as digital activity (if not more important).

A good digital strategy is clearly a vital element of business these days, but you can start to make a success of sales without too much digital activity (or the associated costs).

Some forms of digital activity such as social selling on LinkedIn is used mainly to generate leads as opposed to making sales by digital methods. The idea is to start the discussion and building trust on the digital platform but move the communication to an offline meeting or phone / video call once real interest has been gained.

Once this transition happens, the prospect can be developed into a sale by using the tried-and-tested traditional sales process outlined on page 81 and 82.

The 6 Key Elements of a Hybrid Sales Approach

By using the term 'hybrid sales approach', it is intended to combine the following six things:

- Sales foundation work (building strong sales foundations both online and offline), deciding on your target audience etc. – i.e. following the early points of the 10-point UniC sales planning process
- Digital activity including social media (aligned to sales planning)
- Human interaction **before** the enquiry / buying signal stage (networking and social selling)
- Human interaction at the enquiry / buying signal stage (social selling and face-to-face meetings)
- Local offline promotional activity (sales messaging in local ads, promotional material, events and presentations to local audiences, PR etc.)
- After-sales care – offline and online. Upselling can be a big part of sales success and after-sales care is a vital element of your ongoing sales activity.

This hybrid approach to sales is something I am passionate about, especially for SMEs selling services (or high-value products) within a specific geographic area – e.g. London. Far too many small businesses fail to effectively do this and try to do everything online via social media etc. However, I'm convinced that for most SMEs it's the hybrid approach that is one of the key things that positively impacts sales success.

In my mind, when budget is relatively low, there is nothing more effective at producing sales (for the two types of small businesses this book is aimed at) than human interaction at multiple stages of the process. Remember, people buy people – those they know, like and trust, and when you are talking about service sales or high-value product sales, I think this point is vitally important.

What to Incorporate Into A Hybrid Approach

Below are the key things I think you should be doing to follow a good hybrid approach.

- Building strong sales foundations, including building a good website – the website can be small to begin with, but it needs to be good to be effective
- Sales planning, including understanding the traditional sales process
- Strategic social media activity (on one or maybe two channels) to align with sales planning – one channel must be LinkedIn
- Social selling, primarily using LinkedIn
- SEO-friendly blog writing – this blog content carries value in so many ways
- Business networking – offline and online
- Local events – e.g. low-cost expos – as an exhibitor or visitor
- Sales meetings and intro meetings
- Presentations, locally
- Workshops and webinars – offline and online
- Low-cost local advertising – e.g. magazines, direct mail
- PR – traditional and digital.

To add to this list, as soon as funds allow for a larger website to be built, then ideally, it should be built with strong SEO-friendly foundations. This does not mean money must be spent on ongoing SEO activity straight away. It simply means that the foundations of SEO will be strong from the outset and in place when you do have available funds for ongoing SEO.

The Hybrid Approach – Selling Activity

The 12 points that I have listed on the previous page are the key things that I think need to be done as part of the initial low-cost hybrid approach to sales.

Below are some things that can be done to assist the hybrid activity.

- Create strong social media pages – both personal and business on LinkedIn.
- Find out about all the networking groups you can and create a pool of networking groups to follow on social media so you hear of their events.
- Start going to networking events regularly and building business connections.
- Make a list of your top 10 ideal prospects.
- Plan monthly social media activity ahead of time.
- Plan monthly content writing activity ahead of time.
- Learn about social selling.
- Learn the basics of face-to-face selling.
- Look into costs for local advertising and start some of this if affordable.
- Write at least two blogs per month and plan your blogs quarterly in advance (ideally with help from a high-calibre but low-cost SEO specialist).
- Create a sales toolkit.

Additional Things That Add Value to the Hybrid Approach

Once things are underway with your hybrid selling activity there are certain other things that you can start to put in place to make the process more beneficial.

Below are some of these things:

- **Service clients well** – by providing a good service it will help you with all sorts of things on the sales side. It will help you with word-of-mouth referrals, gaining more work from existing clients in the future, and it will help you obtain recommendations and testimonials.
- **Recommendations and testimonials from clients** – try and collect these for placement on LinkedIn, Google and your own website. The more recommendations and testimonials that you get, the better. This is because good testimonials and recommendations act as proof to others that you can provide a good service. This in turn helps you gain more new sales.
- **Case Studies** – once you have done good work for several clients you can create case studies which can be added to your website and sales literature. These can help build trust and encourage potential prospects to want to use your services.
- **Endorsements** – you can also try to build up more recommendations and endorsements on LinkedIn from people that you work in conjunction with – perhaps suppliers or freelancers.
- **Enter awards** – as soon as you feel that you can do so, then it is a good idea to enter local awards or other business awards for the specific niche that you work in. Even if you don't win these, it can be a good thing to do. If you get shortlisted, for example, the promotional activity that will be done by the people hosting the awards will help you raise your brand

awareness etc. Also, just by entering awards it can give other people more faith in the service that you offer.

- **Appearances** – appear on other people's websites, podcasts, webinars, radio shows etc. if they are highly relevant. This way you don't have to spend too much time on it (not like running your own podcast etc.) but you should benefit from them sharing details of your appearance on social media.

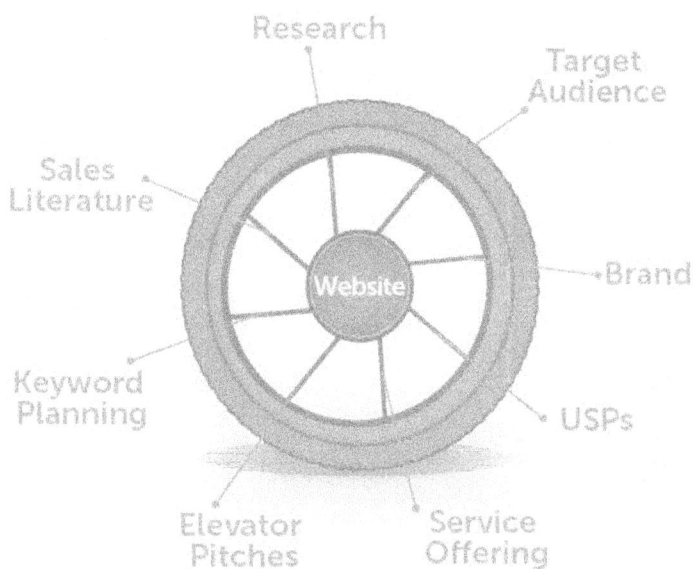

Research

Target Audience

Sales Literature

Website

Brand

Keyword Planning

USPs

Elevator Pitches

Service Offering

CHAPTER 18:

Element 8: Social Media and Social Selling

Social Media

Now that you have seen the 10-point UniC sales planning process explained, it should make a lot more sense to you why going through this type of process is so important for social media activity to work well.

I have already explained the importance of having a good website too. However, having very good LinkedIn landing pages is also a key consideration from a sales perspective.

LinkedIn

LinkedIn is a platform that can add so much value from a sales perspective for so many reasons and it holds an absolute wealth of opportunity if used in the right way.

It's aimed at the business market, so having a very good LinkedIn profile and a business page should help sales immensely as you progress.

I think LinkedIn is a must for most small businesses as it enables small business owners to effectively network with other business owners. It can be used as a great bridge between offline and online activity.

For example, if you go to an offline networking event and meet someone that could be a good connection and maybe a future sales prospect, a great thing to do from a sales perspective is to connect on LinkedIn soon afterwards (or even at the event if you want).

Creating a strong personal profile and a good business page on LinkedIn are very important things to do from a sales perspective as soon as you can.

However, the pages need to be constructed very well and built in line with your sales planning strategy so that they incorporate all the key foundational elements, much like your website.

I will not talk through the ins and outs of creating a strong profile / business page for LinkedIn in this book as there are lots of other books and specialists out there that do that. Nor will I talk about the ins and outs of social selling as that is a whole new subject and, again, there are some great books and specialists out there covering this area.

What I will do is give you a quick summary of what I perceive social selling on LinkedIn to be and why I think it is so important for sales.

Social Selling Overview

I think social media can be one of the most amazing ways to generate sales opportunities if it is used well in line with other sales elements.

I also think 'social selling' on LinkedIn is a great way for small business owners to connect and arrange meetings (online or offline) with other business owners.

As far as I see it, social selling (on LinkedIn) is using this social media channel in a strategic manner that is predominantly 'sales-focused'.

Some of the activities that you can do as part of a social selling strategy are:

- Build connections with people you have met at networking events
- Network with existing connections
- Make new connections – ideally people that meet your target prospect criteria or who meet certain other criteria based around some form of relevancy (e.g. you may wish to connect with people offering similar services to you)
- Liaise with people directly once connected
- Arrange to meet people
- Interact on posts of people you're interested in talking to (comments)
- Make introductions and connect people
- Post in a strategic manner aligned to your sales strategy
- Respond to people that have interacted with you
- Take an initial conversation from LinkedIn into the more traditional-style sales process.

There is much more to it than this, but to summarise I think social selling is much like networking offline.

Unlike video networking where you are stuck in one room or in the hands of the host, with LinkedIn you can essentially move around and go and introduce yourself to people or have a chat with existing contacts. This is just like you would do at an offline networking event.

In my view, the power and potential opportunity from a sales perspective this platform holds for small businesses is immense.

However, like everything I have said throughout, you have to get the basics right first and foremost. With social selling this means:

- sales planning first to get your foundational work right – 10-point UniC sales planning work
- creating a great LinkedIn profile and business page(s)
- building a good initial base of connections
- having a well-planned social selling strategy
- having a good website (even if it is small to begin with)
- setting some KPIs (key performance indicators).

One additional social selling tip that I think is important is not to connect with people just for the sake of it. Taking a quality over quantity approach to connections will have immense value in so many ways.

Too many connections that have no relevancy is likely to muddy your feed and comments, and your direct messages. Like everything else this book has been focused on, social selling for the type of businesses this book is aimed at will work far better if you take a very strategic and highly targeted approach. So, my approach is quality over quantity – it's about being seen and heard by the right people – it is certainly not about vanity metrics or influencer status.

Personally, I think social selling is a complex area, and I think it's probably best to work with specialists who can help you plan your social selling strategy effectively.

However, there is some good info online from specialists, and I have listed some links on the Brand Planning Ltd website at brandplanning.co.uk/social-selling

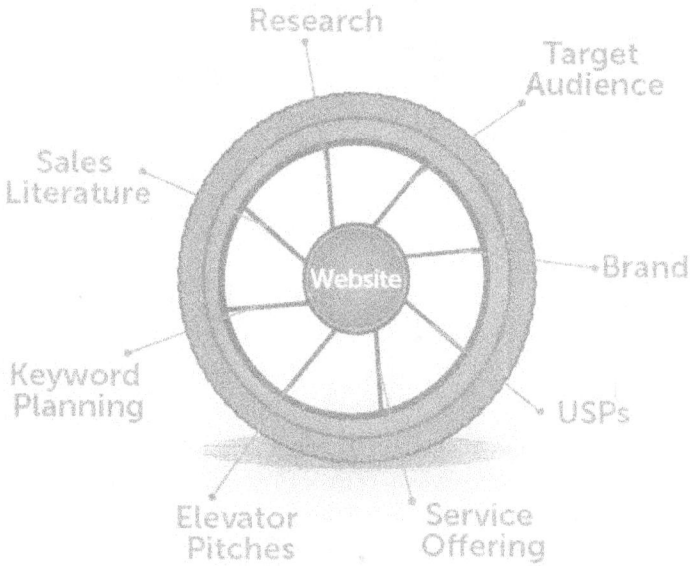

Research

Target Audience

Sales Literature

Website

Brand

Keyword Planning

USPs

Elevator Pitches

Service Offering

CHAPTER 19:

Element 9: SEO Planning and Keyword Planning

One thing I've already explained is that your business website is one of the most powerful sales and marketing tools your business has. Developing your website well should add immense value from a sales perspective.

Whilst I think it is OK to start your hybrid selling approach with only a very small website in place (due to the time and cost implications), the sooner you can get a professional website developed, the better, in my opinion.

A website becomes even more powerful if it's developed to work effectively from an inbound marketing standpoint (i.e. SEO, PPC) and it is beneficial to do the foundational SEO work at the website build stage (even if you are not ready to start paying for SEO help on an ongoing basis).

One important thing to note is that SEO can potentially be done in stages though, which can make it a far more affordable and viable option for small business owners, and this is something people are not always aware of.

For example, you can build the foundations to be SEO-friendly when you first get a professional website built. Then you could go on to add some SEO-friendly blogs slowly but surely over time (possibly with the help of freelance SEO specialists for relatively low cost in comparison to agency work).

You could also do certain other things that will help future SEO, like contributing to good articles on sites that have relevancy that link back to your site.

Then later down the line, when you have the available funds, you could work with a small SEO agency to provide ongoing monthly SEO work. This is where they will apply some more technical and specialist SEO attention to the site each month. They may also do activity like content creation, digital PR and outreach etc. on an ongoing basis.

The thing to be aware of with what I have outlined about doing SEO in stages is that the early work may not show any results until such time that you start having the monthly work done by the agency.

However, all the early work that you have done in terms of building the SEO-friendly foundations and creating ongoing SEO-friendly content for the blogs should have added a lot of value SEO-wise and should prove to be advantageous when you do come to work with an agency. Also, depending how well the initial work is done, and subject to certain other considerations, it could potentially start to work without the need of an agency. Realistically, you'll probably need to work with an SEO specialist for this to be the case though.

It's important to note that SEO usually takes time to take effect, but in my experience it's well worth the work and wait, as enquiries from SEO can be some of the best sales enquiries to receive.

I think inbound marketing (including SEO) is something many small business owners should consider as an integral part of their sales planning strategy. Driving incoming enquiries is one of the main reasons a good website is so important for sales.

Where Does SEO Sit in the Sales and Marketing Mix?

At this point you may be thinking that SEO is a marketing discipline. I don't think it is – I think it is split between sales, marketing, and digital development.

The sales side of SEO is what is aligned to sales planning and the initial website development work, and includes areas like keyword research, content planning and the navigational system of the site. For SEO to be successful from a sales standpoint, it needs to be based very heavily around your sales objectives and foundational sales element work, particularly keyword planning. For more information on keyword planning go to page 174.

The digital development activity is what I would class as the more technical elements of SEO. So, this includes things like site loading times and tagging etc.

The marketing side would be all the things that a typical digital / SEO agency would do monthly to improve SEO on an ongoing basis. This is things like outreach, digital PR, content distribution, link building and possibly the creation of more technical elements of copy like meta tags. They would also look at the growth strategy (which would need to be a mix of sales and marketing focus).

SEO Tips

Below I've listed my thoughts relating to SEO for small business owners in the B2B sector.

- SEO enquiries make great sales enquiries as they drive visitors to your site when they are specifically looking for keywords related to your business – this often means they are already in 'buying mode'.
- SEO is complex, but it can really help boost sales. It can potentially be applied in an affordable way by applying different elements of SEO at different stages of brand development.
- SEO is fantastic for some SMEs and not a viable option for others. I think it tends to be a better option for service businesses or high-value product businesses, and not as good for businesses selling low-cost items. Although clever SEO specialists can generally find strategies to make it work for most businesses.
- SEO is generally viewed as being expensive by SME owners. Whilst it does carry a higher cost than many forms of marketing (because of the complexity of doing it), the results will usually outweigh expense if it is planned and implemented well in line with sales planning. When done well, SEO can deliver a fantastic return on investment and one that keeps improving as time progresses.
- Small businesses often consider SEO way too late in their brand development – this is because a big element of SEO (i.e. SEO foundations) needs to be done at the web build or website redesign stage. Planning SEO as early as possible (even if you don't do much SEO activity to begin with) can be so helpful as time progresses. If you don't do it at the web build stage, you may have to redesign your website when you do want to start doing SEO.

- The sooner an SME starts SEO the better – for several reasons. SEO takes time, sites tend to become more responsive to SEO over time etc.
- If a small business can't afford an SEO agency, then by working with SEO strategists, some ongoing SEO work could be done relatively cheaply – e.g. blog content.
- There are potentially various elements of SEO work that SMEs can do themselves if they work with SEO strategists.
- Good keyword planning is pivotal for small business SEO success, but keyword planning is a lot more specialised than it sounds and it's probably best to use specialists if you want good results.
- Having a very good understanding of your target market, your competition and your niche are important aspects of a good SEO strategy.
- SEO activity should be closely aligned to sales planning for best results.
- There is synergy between SEO and PPC, which can have some benefits from a sales perspective, as potentially PPC could drive sales leads more quickly than SEO if landing pages have been built well already as part of the SEO foundation work. This can sometimes be a great option while you are waiting for SEO to take effect.
- I believe your SEO strategy should sit at the heart of your content strategy if you are looking for long-term gain from incoming enquiries.
- Content written for SEO can be repurposed for other things, so the work put into SEO helps all sorts of areas.
- Gaining results from SEO is not generally something that happens quickly, and it should be viewed as a longer-term method of promotion. It tends to require ongoing work / investment too. There are no guarantees for success, but when applied well by specialists, SEO can produce superb results which have a positive impact on sales.

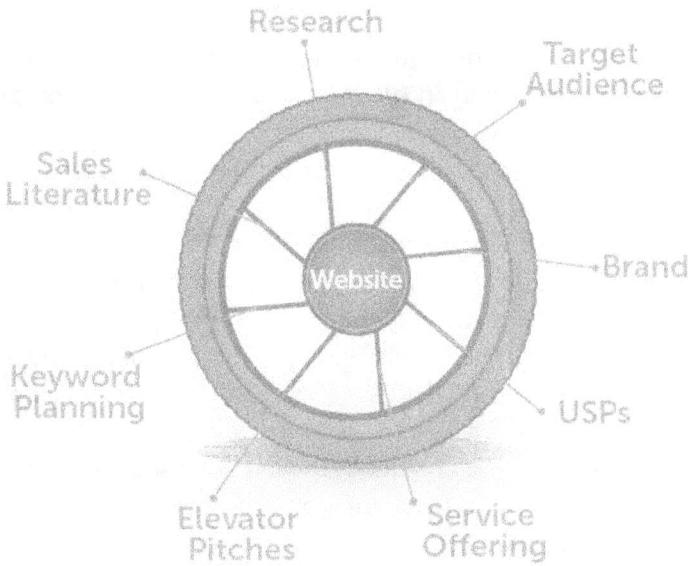

Research

Target Audience

Sales Literature

Website

Brand

Keyword Planning

USPs

Elevator Pitches

Service Offering

CHAPTER 20:

Element 10: Website Planning and Content

A problem I encounter a lot is that it seems that, often, people don't realise how important a website is and what a positive impact a good website can have on your business!

A website sits centrally to so many other elements of sales and marketing. It is such an important tool for business growth and sales. When funds allow, I think most SMEs should have a professional website built that includes strong foundations from a sales, marketing and SEO standpoint.

You only have to look back to the list on page 134 that shows where your domain name appears to see why a website is so centrally placed in terms of the sales, marketing and digital mix. This is because the domain name and the website are linked to each other. So, wherever your domain name appears, it can lead people to your website.

The major difference between offline and online sales, is that online there is often no salesperson to entice the customer to view products, or to liaise directly with the customer to ask questions, find out their needs, handle objections or close the sale.

These are key elements of the sales process, and they are still important in digital sales. Finding ways to incorporate these elements into your website is one reason why a good website is so important.

It's also why focusing on a niche area is so important. After all, a website cannot be all things to all people, so developing your website around your specialist area (niche) can be very beneficial.

How Much Does a Professional Website Cost?

The cost of having a good website planned and built professionally can vary quite a lot. I estimate the design and build will vary from about £2000 upwards for a 10-page website.

The more pages and functionality you want, the more expensive it is likely to be.

If you want to include SEO planning and professional copywriting too (which is often advisable), then the cost is likely to be nearer £4000 to £6000 or more.

This may sound expensive, but the value a professionally designed website can deliver is immense.

If your website is planned, designed and developed well by specialists who know what they are doing, then it should act as a central hub to house key foundational sales elements. This should assist greatly with sales as outlined in the sales planning wheel diagram on page 107.

It should act as an information point / brochure, and an ever-growing content hub. Perhaps most importantly, it should essentially act like an online salesperson alongside being the landing point for so many other forms of promotional activity.

> I think that a website should be viewed as an investment that is going to help the business progress greatly both in the short-term and long-term. I cannot stress enough what a valuable sales tool a good website is for small business owners.

Website Planning

To generate good incoming sales enquiries from a website, you need to generate traffic (i.e. visitors), but there is no point in generating traffic if your website is not well designed. First impressions count, so having a good design is vital.

Similarly, there is little point generating traffic if the website is hard to navigate, does not function well, is low on content, or looks like it has not been professionally built, because these things put visitors off from making enquiries.

In fact, as much as I highly value a good website, I think it's probably better to have no website at all than to have a very poor website. This is because a poor website can potentially do damage to your image and your brand / business from a sales stance.

A website needs to have visitors and have a good design, structure and various other things (listed on page 241) to work well from a sales standpoint.

Website Development Considerations

There is a lot that goes into website planning, but to start off with, here are 3 key things that you need to think about first and foremost when having a website developed.

- Who is your audience?
- What are you selling to them?
- What sales messages do you want the website to relay?

If you follow the 10-point UniC sales planning process, these types of questions (and similar ones) will have been answered as part of earlier sales foundations work, before you get to the website planning stage.

Then there are several other questions you should think about prior to a website build — as these are the areas you will want web developers to work on when they build a site for you.

- How are people going to find it?
- What will they think of it visually?
- How easy will it be for them to use and find their way around?
- When they do find it, will it make a good first impression and provide informative information that encourages visitors to want to know more?
- How will visitors make enquiries?
- What can you offer that will encourage people to interact and want to sign up to newsletters etc?
- What questions will it answer?
- How are you going to relay your key messages and selling points effectively?

A decent-sized 'sales-focused' website that is professionally designed and built should in my opinion incorporate the following:

- Good design
- Easy-to-use navigation system
- Homepage
- UX (user experience)
- CRO (conversion rate optimisation)
- 'About Us' page
- Tech elements
- Local landing pages – to help gain local enquiries
- Services pages – showing what you do
- A blog section
- A testimonial section
- An FAQ section
- 'Contact Us' page
- Footer text, which includes page links and legal requirements (e.g. Ts & Cs - best to consult with specialists).

Your website should also be written extremely well from a copywriting perspective, and this ideally requires a specialist copywriter. This is because good website copywriting will incorporate all sorts of things from a sales, marketing and SEO stance, whilst ensuring the copy is useful and informative for the ideal user.

Design

The design of your website and the visual impact it delivers is one of the first things people are likely to see in relation to your business, and first impressions are incredibly important!

The design should incorporate all the branding considerations and represent the brand well.

The Navigation

I explained this earlier but am explaining again as it has real relevance and is important to understand because the website sits so centrally from a sales perspective.

If you think of a website like a tree, with the homepage as the trunk and all the top-level pages (say 10 of them) leading from the trunk being main branches. From each main branch, smaller branches can grow.

So, for example, as time progresses and you develop the site further, then the main services page branch (for example) could have links put on it to smaller branches (i.e. other pages that lead from it showing each of your individual services). This will enable you to start building very well, from a general website growth perspective, but also from an SEO and PPC perspective.

From an SEO perspective, if each page that is built is planned with SEO in mind and keyword research is done prior to the page build, then the site can be built so that (a) it has strong SEO foundations with the initial pages and (b) there is a lot of scope for SEO growth. This is just one of the reasons why it is so very important to think about keywords and SEO planning prior to building a website and not afterwards.

Homepage

Your homepage is the main entry point of your website, so it needs to look good, and ideally it should have links to some of the other main sections, so that these are easily accessible from the homepage as well as the navigation bar.

UX (user experience)

This relates to the navigation, page layout, ease of use and visual impact from a user's perspective. The site needs to be easy to use and easy to get around – so if you equate this to a wayfinding system in the real world, the equivalent of that essentially needs to be in place on a website.

CRO (conversion rate optimisation)

CRO means conversion rate optimisation and relates to the buttons, graphics and links that are in place that encourage users to interact and make enquiries. These are often known as 'call to action' elements.

About Us

The 'About Us' section is an important section because:

- it can potentially help from an SEO perspective
- it's likely to be one of the first areas that people look at to decide whether they like your company and want to know more or link to you
- it's a place to say more about you, your background, the company, and your company USPs and brand identity.

The Technical Side of Things

Good web developers will know what to do to make sure a site is built well from a technical perspective – this includes looking at things like site loading speed, where the site is hosted, technical tagging, security etc. and ensuring it works well on different browsers and screen sizes (e.g. mobile). These things need to be done well so that the website runs as smoothly as possible, and many tech elements help with SEO.

Local Pages

Local pages – i.e. 'a local Bromley page' – to use for PPC and social media activity (primarily) for the local area is a good idea for many websites, especially for businesses selling services in a specific local area. This does not need to be in the main navigation though, and it could be tucked away somewhere on the site (e.g. as a link from the contact page). It's more about you driving traffic to it, than about the user seeing it easily from the main site, although these things can potentially help with local SEO too.

Services Pages

The main services pages should be well-thought-out landing pages around very specific services relevant to your business. If you want the services pages to include prices, they can, but that is up to you.

There should be a main services page about your services generally and then at least one or two pages about individual services.

The Blog Section

The blog section is a really important area to get right from a growth perspective, as the application of regular blogs is a way that you can start to enhance SEO and your social media activity.

Client Testimonials and Case Studies

Testimonials help to build trust. If you can keep adding testimonials that is a good thing to do as these show potential prospects what a good job you have done for other clients and gives them more faith in your service offering.

It could be a good idea to do a couple of case studies, if you could get clients to agree to you doing this, as this would add a sense of trust / confidence.

FAQs

The frequently asked questions section can be a good opportunity to answer the typical questions that ideal prospects are likely to ask, whilst alleviating some of the concerns relating to the pain points they have.

Contact Us

Using a mobile phone number on a website does not give a good impression in my opinion, as it makes you look small, and some people can view it as looking unprofessional. It could be worth looking into getting a business number and there are various ways to do this.

No office address? This does not look good either, plus you really need an office address to add to the site and directories etc. and there are some legalities to consider here too.

Footer and Legal Requirements

The footer of the website usually contains links to key pages and is another way for users to navigate the site.

Also, there are certain legal considerations or requirements that you'll need to think about when having a website developed, which include such things as incorporating website terms and conditions, and how you should display your company details. Links to these elements tend to appear in the footer of the website. It's something to be mindful of and it's important to speak to specialists about these things.

There are various other legal considerations that you'll need to be aware of, if you want people to sign up for newsletters and send enquiries.

There are many big organisations that help start-ups and small businesses, and they often provide information and / or assistance for these legal areas. These organisations can be a very good starting point for help with the legal aspects. A list of some of these organisations can be found at brandplanning.co.uk/small-business-support

SEO Foundations

Making sure that your core web pages are built well from an SEO perspective using good keywords is important. However, keyword usage is just one consideration, and there are all sorts of other things to take into account when building SEO-friendly websites. So, it's important to work with specialists on this side of things.

Website Content

One of the things that the search engines look for to decide how good a website is from an SEO perspective is the amount of quality content it has.

Content planning is something that needs to be discussed in detail with specialists too, as whilst you may start with a relatively small website, you want to be able to grow it which involves good content planning.

As an overview, website content could take the form of blogs, web pages, eBooks, video etc. Planning a strategy that meets the following criteria is what would be good to look at:

- SEO-friendly content around good keyword research
- Evergreen content (content that does not go out of date)
- 'How to' content
- Content for multi-channel use
- Content where snippets can be used on social media
- Long articles
- Regular blogging

Why Not Just Have Social Media Pages? – It's So Much Cheaper!

A lot of small business owners seem to be of the misguided opinion that they don't need to spend money or time developing a good website. Often, this is because they believe having a social media presence is enough, and that it's a lot cheaper.

I think this is both a naïve and risky route to take. The points I have listed on page 95 show you why a website is so valuable. But if this is not enough to convince you, on the next two pages are a few reasons why I do not think it is a good idea to put the emphasis on social media.

Please note, I do think it's OK to just use social media pages (particularly LinkedIn) and maybe a very small website to begin with, perhaps for the first year or two. Doing things this way actually forms part of the initial hybrid approach I suggest taking because I know that the cost of professional web development is too prohibitive for some businesses in the early years.

However, by following the 10-point UniC sales planning process, you should start generating sales from several different methods.

Once sales start coming in and generating revenue, then you should be able to invest in a professional website, and at this point I think most small business owners should make this a priority!

Reasons to Avoid Just Using Social Media Pages

- Don't put your eggs all in one basket – especially when you don't own the basket! This is probably the most important point, as social media platforms can change rules, disappear or block accounts, and you have no control over this. Imagine if you put all your eggs in one social media basket (as it were), only to find out that you no longer had any access to the basket, or it had disappeared overnight. I think that's a scary thought for any business owner who is putting too much emphasis on social media.
- What you write on social media quickly fades into the ether and is often of little value to you a day or two after posting, whereas website content can stay in place for years.
- Website content becomes more valuable over time, whereas social media content tends to lose value over time.
- There is often limited space in social media posts, but on your website you have much more flexibility with the number of words.
- Whilst certain social media posts can potentially add some value from an SEO perspective, search engine optimisation techniques are better applied to your own website for long-term gain.
- It's often hard to get clear insight into all the things a company does from their social media pages as they can be a bit disjointed – a website is often much easier to navigate and joins things up better.
- It's hard to direct visitors to different sections of social media accounts to see information. This tends to be much easier

with websites because you can direct people to different sections of the site via different URL suffixes:

- For example, the 'services' button goes to the page of the Brand Planning Ltd website that shows all the services, which can be found here – brandplanning.co.uk/marketing-services
- Whereas if I just want to inform people of the workshops, I can send them here – brandplanning.co.uk/sales-workshops

What Stops Business Owners Investing in a Website?

There are several reasons small business owners don't invest in a good website.

Some of these are listed below.

- **They don't think they need one**. I've already explained why I think they do need a website if they want to do well at sales.
- **They think it will be too expensive**. It is relatively expensive for a small business owner but it's probably one of the best investments you're likely to make in your business journey. So, I think the sooner you can invest in a professional website, the better.
- **They don't know where to start**. There are usually all sorts of small digital agencies in local areas. I suggest contacting a few of these initially or asking around locally for recommendations when at networking events, or via LinkedIn.
- **They think it will be too complex**. Good web design and web development are quite complex, but if you use specialists, they will be able to help you through the whole process.

- **They think it will be too time-consuming**. It will be time-consuming, but having a professional website should save a lot of time, energy and money. Once in place, a good website should help you meet your sales objectives, raise awareness and promote your business effectively on an ongoing basis.
- **They don't realise what value it will bring them**. I have explained some of this already, but below I have listed 20 reasons why I believe a good website is so beneficial.

20 Reasons Why a Professionally Developed Website is So Beneficial

1. Most forms of sales and marketing and promotional activity will lead to your website.
2. If the website foundations are built to be SEO-friendly at the outset it will help SEO in the future.
3. It acts as an online salesperson by doing the following:
   - Informing people about your USPs, values, team etc
   - Informing people about your services
   - Telling your business story
   - Answering FAQs
   - Building trust with testimonials, case studies etc
   - Encouraging enquiries.
4. Content that you add to your website stays in place forever (if you want), so content added today could potentially benefit you for years to come.
5. It becomes a content hub, and you can direct people to find specific pieces of content. If the site is built well, the content should also be searchable via a search mechanism on the website.
6. It's a great sales tool for you to use offline and online.
7. It can be used as a display tool, for events, presentations etc.
8. You can house videos and podcasts on your website.

9. It provides a space for you to create and promote an online product range – e.g. courses, eBooks.
10. It enables you to do other forms of inbound marketing like PPC (pay per click).
11. It makes your business look far more professional.
12. It allows you to publish prices and rate cards (if you want) so visitors can gain an idea of your pricing.
13. A good website will work for you 24 / 7. Even when you are sleeping it can be promoting your business and essentially selling for you.
14. If SEO foundations are built well, you could potentially gain some SEO traction without having to work with agencies – by adding SEO-friendly blogs etc.
15. Your website will help all sorts of people find you, not just potential prospects. This could include people looking for strategic partnerships. A well-designed, professional-looking website can open the door to all sorts of opportunities.
16. It allows you to produce blogs regularly which can add value in so many ways.
17. You can mention your website in social media posts and it adds value to all sorts of things you do on social media.
18. It enables you to end your elevator pitch with your web address.
19. It builds brand awareness.
20. It can help you drive visitors from audio promotion (e.g. podcasts and audio sessions on social media).

There are so many reasons why it makes sense to invest in a professionally built website. The most important reason is because your website and your brand are interlocked and will sit centrally to everything else that you do online and offline to promote your business!

In my opinion, this makes your website (and domain / brand name) the most powerful sales and marketing tool that you could possibly have.

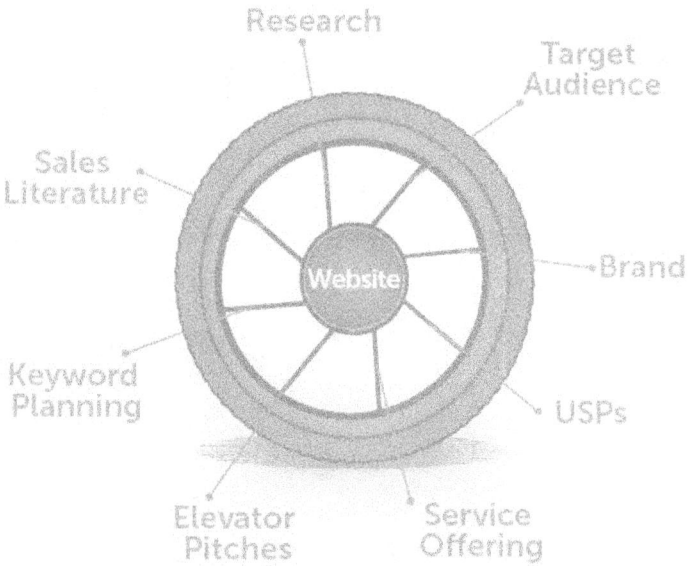

CHAPTER 21:

The First Four Promotional Routes to Follow for Sales Success

There are many different marketing and promotional routes that small businesses could take, but lots of these have quite substantial costs that need to be invested monthly for them to deliver good results.

For example, SEO, PPC, social media advertising, and exhibiting at / sponsoring big events are all good ways to generate quality incoming leads, but they cost money to implement and run.

Also, there are several methods of marketing that are potentially low cost, but these take time to do well, and one thing small business owners are often short of is time.

Things like video marketing, podcast creation, email marketing, content marketing (through the creation of eBooks) etc. are examples of these low-cost opportunities that could work very well when a business owner has sufficient time to invest in doing them properly.

However, if they are not planned and implemented effectively, or done consistently on an ongoing basis, I think returns from this type of activity can often be poor. So having the time to invest in these areas is of paramount importance for them to deliver good results. Until then, using other low-cost promotional methods may be more beneficial.

Choosing What Promotional Activity to Do

The main purpose of the 10-point UniC sales planning process is to help people create strong sales foundations and a good sales strategy, so that the money they go on to put into sales, marketing and promotional activity produces the best return on investment as quickly as possible.

Deciding on the right target audience and niche are two areas of the 10-point UniC sales planning process I believe are very important to plan well. Whilst the foundational work for these elements is what I would class as sales work, there is a big overlap with marketing, and ideally the future marketing / promotional side needs to be given some serious thought during the sales planning stage.

I think the 10-point UniC sales planning process has a secondary stage (which I am just touching on very briefly in this chapter). This involves finding ways in which to get strong sales messages in front of your target audience and it is the vital next step of the sales planning process. This promotional activity is likely to require a combination of sales, marketing, advertising and social media activity for best results.

It is the planning of a good strategy for promotional activity that will deliver sales enquiries on an ongoing basis – both from outreach and incoming activity. By outreach, I mean any method where you are being proactive in sourcing sales prospects and developing sales leads – whereas incoming activity is where these come to you.

There is a lot involved in doing promotional activity effectively for low cost and there is a lot of choice of what can be done.

A good plan needs to be put together for this as you will not be able to do everything all at once. So, a plan needs to be devised of what to do and when, and this needs to be tailored to your individual business.

All sorts of things need to be considered during this promotional planning stage, such as an events calendar, the budget available, and the resources available for content creation and implementation work.

Networking, Social Selling and Social Media Marketing

There are four initial promotional routes to market that I think are the most accessible and cost-effective methods for small businesses to start doing first and foremost.

The first three of these are:

- Networking – which I identify as being a cross between sales and marketing
- Social selling – which is sales focused, and I'd class this as a cross between sales and networking
- Social media marketing – which is a form of marketing.

> I have already talked about networking a lot in the book, and
> I think a heavy emphasis needs to be put on this and social
> selling. Combining these two promotional activities with all
> the elements of the 10-point UniC sales planning process,
> and undertaking some social media marketing, is what all
> small business owners should be able to do cost effectively
> to get them off to a great start, sales-wise.

With social media marketing activity, I think it's usually better for
SMEs to focus on just one, or maybe two platforms, and learn to
use these well. One of these platforms needs to be LinkedIn.

Some businesses may benefit from using another platform too,
and which one this is should be decided in line with the target
audience and niche area of focus – as the platforms differ in many
ways, and different platforms will be more appropriate for different
businesses.

The Fourth Key Route to Market – Local Promotion

A lot of small businesses just focus on servicing clients within
a local area. When I say that, a local area could be fairly wide
though – i.e. London could be a local area for the purpose of the
point I am making.

But many businesses will concentrate on an even more defined
local area, say South London.

There is a wealth of opportunity in terms of low-cost local
promotional activity, but this is something that many SMEs seem
to overlook – choosing instead to focus heavily on social media
marketing because it's free.

Whilst I think social media marketing adds value, it can be problematic to focus all your energy and resources on this for several reasons, including the following:

- Social media marketing is not actually free when you account for time costs and costs of content creation etc.
- Unless you pay for ads or do social selling, it is hard to target locally with social media marketing – so a lot of people that see posts won't have the potential of becoming clients as they are the wrong audience.
- It can be quite hard to drive people from social media marketing activity to your website (harder than some other forms of promotional activity, anyway), as people do not want to leave the social media platform. Because your website is essentially the main online tool that can act as a salesperson, this is another good reason why social media marketing is not the best option to plough lots of time into.
- If you just focus on social media marketing, you are putting all your eggs in a basket you don't own or have control of, which I think is a risky thing to do.

I think spending small amounts of budget on different forms of local promotional activity, ensuring your web address is used clearly on all methods, is a much better way for small businesses to get in front of the right target audience – i.e. people who will be the right people to show an interest and, ultimately, go on to buy services.

Types of Local / Niche Promotional Opportunities (Relatively Low Cost)

- Ads in trade mags, for your niche
- Branded workwear
- Business cards

- Directory listings – local
- Door drops
- Editorial articles
- Flyers
- Joining local business organisations
- Listings or guest blogs on prominent local websites, or sites aligned to your niche
- Local ads – magazines / newspapers
- Local adverts – in retail outlets and similar
- Local events – advertising
- Local events – delivery
- Local events – exhibitor
- Podcast appearances – on podcasts relevant to your niche
- Local PR
- Local radio
- Local search
- Local sponsorship opportunities
- Newsletter inclusion
- Outdoor advertising
- Promotional items – e.g. branded mugs, stationery
- Pull-up banners
- Referrals
- Roundtables
- Speaking
- Strategic partnership promotion
- Vehicle advertising
- Webinars
- Workshops.

I think combining the 10-point UniC sales planning process with the four initial promotional routes to market I have outlined, and a well-planned strategy for promotional activity, is the best way forward for SMEs with low budgets.

Blog Planning Strategy

I think blogs can be a great method to generate traffic from SEO in the future (once SEO work is applied), and blogs can be used in several other ways to help generate awareness. The content of blogs can also be repurposed for all sorts of other forms of promotion and digital activity.

I therefore think it is a very good idea for SMEs to have a blog planning and writing programme in place as soon as possible too, and for them to produce regular monthly blogs, no matter how small the initial website.

Ideally, it is great to work with an SEO specialist on this so the blogs can be developed to be SEO-friendly from the outset. However, the main thing is to write interesting content about your niche area.

Good-quality blogs should be beneficial in a multitude of ways both short-term and long-term. If they are not SEO-friendly from the outset, this is not a major problem as they should be able to be enhanced and made SEO-friendly at a later date.

Achieving Sales Success

As you can see, the activity that I propose being the best form of initial promotional activity for small businesses with low budgets is very much a hybrid approach, as mentioned in previous chapters.

It is also a combination of highly targeted sales, marketing, social media and advertising activity, which is all sales-focused and aligned to the target audience and the 10-point UniC sales planning process every step of the way.

EMMA MEHEUX | www.salesbeforemarketing.com

It also encompasses thinking about the foundations of future SEO with several elements of the activity. For example, the blogs will help SEO in the future – as will links gained from other quality sites, which will happen naturally because of some of the promotional activity (e.g. speaker appearances) and any PR gained.

By starting to do some SEO work early on, it makes it easier to implement a full SEO strategy later down the line. It should also help to produce results from SEO more quickly once SEO specialists start working on things in the future.

> As part of any promotional activity, one key thing to be mindful of at all stages is your brand, as the continuity and consistency of your branding needs to be maintained. After all, your branding should be like a fine chain that runs through every aspect of what you do online and offline, helping you raise brand awareness on an ongoing basis.

CHAPTER 22:
Summary

The purpose of this book and the 10-point UniC sales planning process is to help entrepreneurs and small business owners start to take big steps forward with 'sales'.

Now you have read the book, hopefully you will have gained more insight and clarity about sales and feel encouraged to start devising your strategy for sales progression.

You should also now understand why I believe so strongly that it should always be **sales before marketing**.

I hope you feel ready to start stepping forward with sales and putting some of the elements of the 10-point UniC sales planning process into action.

Below is a reminder of some of the key things the book has covered.

- What sales is
- Why sales is so important
- Why it's sales before marketing
- Why not to shy away from sales
- What makes strong sales foundations
- How to sell effectively both online and offline
- Why strong sales foundations are so important
- How to develop your business in a sales-focused way

- How to take a hybrid approach to sales (offline and online)
- How to gain sales enquiries by inbound sales and marketing activity
- How to follow a cyclical system of sales and marketing, starting with sales
- Why having a high-quality, SEO-friendly website is so good for improving sales
- What sales-focused promotional activity to do as your first four routes to market.

Costs of the 10-point UniC Sales Planning Process

One subject that I have not covered in this book is the cost associated with this sales planning process.

This is partly because sales planning, website development, SEO, and the key areas of promotional activity I have mentioned will all vary in price depending on the volume of work required, and other considerations. Pricing is also likely to change over time.

Detailed information about the costings related to the 10-Point UniC Sales Planning Process can instead be found at the Sales Before Marketing website. You will also find several other free resources here that you may find useful.

salesbeforemarketing.com/resources

About the Author

Emma Meheux is a sales and marketing consultant, and SEO specialist. She is the founder of Brand Planning Ltd, a sales-focused strategic planning consultancy for SMEs.

Emma has over 30 years' experience in sales and marketing and has held senior roles for several well-known brands. She has also worked for / in conjunction with many digital agencies.

She's extremely well connected with senior executives and business leaders throughout the digital, media, marketing, retail, publishing and small business sectors, with over 2500 quality connections on LinkedIn.

Emma regularly speaks at events about sales and marketing. Details of the speaking sessions she provides can be seen here – brandplanning.co.uk/business-speaker

Alongside speaking at events, and to in-house teams, Emma provides a range of roundtable opportunities and workshops through Brand Planning Ltd that could be of interest to readers. Details of the workshops can be found here – brandplanning.co.uk/sales-workshops

Contact Emma

Find out more about Emma, her work and the services provided by Brand Planning at brandplanning.co.uk

You can find information about a newsletter here too. brandplanning.co.uk/newsletter

You can also email info@brandplanning.co.uk

Or follow Emma on LinkedIn at linkedin.com/in/brandplanning

REQUEST FROM THE AUTHOR:
Please Don't Forget to Share

Good books take a very long time to write and an even longer time to produce and market effectively. This book has been self-published with the help of specialists and there are costs involved with that – so writing a book like this is a big step for a small business owner like Emma.

In this book, Emma has done her best to share insightful information gained from over 30 years of sales experience, which should help readers improve sales, and she really hopes you enjoyed the read.

She has one request for readers – if you liked the book, please share posts about it on your social media channels, give reviews, or link to brandplanning.co.uk or salesbeforemarketing.com from your website. These things help writers immensely.

Doing this should also help enable more entrepreneurs and small business owners hear about the book, so they can read it and have a better chance of achieving sales success.

Positive responses to this request are also likely to encourage Emma to write more useful information, and maybe even more books, to help you and other small business owners improve sales and marketing activity.

There is more information about how to help here.

salesbeforemarketing.com/promotion

Positivity Poems

As outlined in this book, business can be tough, and looking after your wellbeing and mental health is so important for all entrepreneurs and business owners. This is something Emma is passionate about, and she wants to help raise awareness of this.

Emma is a poet as well as a writer, and she writes a lot of poetry about mental health and wellbeing.

Much of this poetry is written with the stresses that business owners go through in mind.

Emma often posts her poems on LinkedIn to provide some uplifting words to the small business community. She has also started doing poetry readings. For those readers who like poetry, Emma has included five of her poems here.

If you want to book Emma for a poetry reading, please visit salesbeforemarketing.com/poetry-speaker

Energise Your Mind

When the world seems too tough,
And stress is all around,
Take a long deep breath of air,
As you walk across the ground.

Look up at the clouds above,
Watch the wind blow through the trees,
Listen to the birds in song,
Feel the gentle, calming breeze.

Immerse yourself in nature,
Feel the strength of its caress,
Let it energise your mind,
And alleviate your stress.

Small Steps Lead to Big Strides

The small steps matter,
Every small step counts,
Each small step that you make,
Will help you surmount.

The obstacles in your path,
The hurdles in your way,
The challenges of business life,
The stress of day-to-day.

Be proud of the steps you take,
Count each one as you go,
Visualise your line of steps,
Like footprints in the snow.

Enjoy the Journey

If you feel you're on a mountain,
And it's hard to reach the top,
Slow right down and take a breath,
Then, look around and stop.

There's no need to reach the summit,
You don't have to aim so high,
You can just enjoy the journey,
And let others pass you by.

It's not a sprint to reach success,
Nor a race to supersede,
It's just a climb to find your place,
And accomplish what you need.

Rewards Require Resilience

Sometimes, the stronger we are,
The deeper and harder we fall,
It's those who pull themselves up again,
Who are the bravest and strongest of all.

An Ever-changing Tapestry

Remember, business is like life,
An ever-changing tapestry of events,
What you change today may impact tomorrow,
What impacts today may change tomorrow,
All you can ever do is your best,
And your best is good enough.

You can find out more about the poetry Emma writes by visiting:

salesbeforemarketing.com/poetry

Notes

www.ingramcontent.com/pod-product-compliance
Lightning Source LLC
Chambersburg PA
CBHW071337210326
41597CB00015B/1476